Big Ideas in Primary Science

Understanding the Climate Crisis

Peter Loxley

Routledge
Taylor & Francis Group

LONDON AND NEW YORK

Cover image: curioustiger / istock

First published 2023
by Routledge
4 Park Square, Milton Park, Abingdon, Oxon OX14 4RN

and by Routledge
605 Third Avenue, New York, NY 10158

Routledge is an imprint of the Taylor & Francis Group, an informa business

British Library Cataloguing-in-Publication Data
A catalogue record for this book is available from the British Library

Library of Congress Cataloging-in-Publication Data
Names: Loxley, Peter, author.
Title: Big ideas in primary science : understanding the climate crisis / Peter Loxley.
Description: Abingdon, Oxon ; New York, NY : Routledge, 2022. |
    Includes bibliographical references and index.
Identifiers: LCCN 2022009976 | ISBN 9780367762896 (hardback) |
    ISBN 9780367762902 (paperback) | ISBN 9781003166276 (ebook)
Subjects: LCSH: Science—Study and teaching (Primary)—Great Britain. |
    Climatic changes—Study and teaching (Primary)—Great Britain.
Classification: LCC LB1532 .L68 2022 | DDC 372.35/044—dc23/eng/20220425
LC record available at https://lccn.loc.gov/2022009976

ISBN: 978-0-367-76289-6 (hbk)
ISBN: 978-0-367-76290-2 (pbk)
ISBN: 978-1-003-16627-6 (ebk)

DOI: 10.4324/9781003166276

Typeset in Frutiger
by Apex CoVantage, LLC

CONTENTS

FIGURES

All the figures which are not individually credited are sourced from iStock collections.

ACKNOWLEDGEMENT

I would like to thank Bruce and Molly at Routledge for their help and encouraging words. I would also like to say a very special thank you to my wife, Anna, for her research and the many valuable ideas she has contributed to the book.

climate crisis · glacier melt · methane emissions · drought ·
single-use plastic · acid rain · habitat fragmentation · reef loss ·
ocean acidification · permafrost thawing · bush fires · food waste ·
ice cap melt · food air miles · coral bleaching · frequent flooding ·
changing phenology · warming seas · greenhouse effect ·
pollinator decline · excess landfill · fossil fuel extraction · ice loss ·
global shift in migration patterns · micro plastic pollution ·
altered weather patterns · CO_2 emissions · sea level rise ·
black carbon · throw-away economy · carbon footprint ·
over-consumption · coastal erosion · island nations drowning ·
wood burners · food air miles · bio-accumulation · fast fashion ·
fracking · increasing land temperatures · habitat loss ·
accelerated deforestation · carbon fuel emissions · climate denial ·
urban heat islands · demand for out-of-season food ·
fossil fuel combustion · carbon-emitting energy sources ·
threatened species · climate change refugees · green-washing ·
destruction of indigenous peoples' lifestyles · over-tilling the soil ·
meat production · frequent fliers · vehicle exhaust fumes ·
impermeable parking areas · peat-bed destruction ·
exploitation of finite resources · loss of crops and animals ·
increased severity in wet and dry seasons · beach slumping ·
extreme weather impact on infrastructure · shrinking ice packs ·
longer sea ice-free seasons · emergence of invasive species ·
weaker ice to travel on · biodiversity collapse · no Planet B ·

CHAPTER 1
WORKING TOWARDS BIG IDEAS

Schoolchildren around the world have led the way when it comes to taking climate action, consequently providing role models for many of their elders. What they have achieved is remarkable, in many cases without the benefit of climate education being taught in their schools.

The purpose of this book is to provide help and encouragement for primary teachers to integrate big ideas about the climate crisis into their curriculum. The content of the book is most suitable for children aged between 7 and 11 years, and is consistent with primary school curricula in England, Wales, Scotland, and Northern Ireland. Although the learning activities set out in the book are mainly related to science, there are also opportunities for children to develop skills and understanding from other curriculum areas, such as geography, design technology, and art.

Learning throughout the book is based on four big ideas. By making the ideas their own, children can develop informed ways of thinking about issues related to global warming and climate change, and feel empowered to act in ways which can make a difference.

Big ideas

Ch. 3 and 4: Processes that occur on the Earth's surface and in its atmosphere combine to shape its weather and its climate.

Ch. 5: Climate change is a long-term shift in average weather patterns across the world, caused by human activity.

Ch. 6 and 7: Climate change is accelerating faster than expected and is threatening natural ecosystems and the fate of humanity.

Ch. 8 and 9: We need to change the way we live in order to reduce carbon emissions to net zero and prevent irreparable damage to our planet.

Topics

Teaching and learning is focused on the following seven topics:

- Chapter 3: Weather
- Chapter 4: Climate
- Chapter 5: Climate change
- Chapter 6: Impact of climate crisis on our lives
- Chapter 7: Impact of the climate crisis on wildlife

- Chapter 8: The world we must create
- Chapter 9: Taking climate action

Each topic is structured in two parts. Part 1 provides *subject knowledge*, which teachers can use to help teach the topic, and Part 2 sets out *models of good practice*, which provide ideas and activities teachers can use to organise children's learning towards the big ideas. The *models of good practice* are not intended for use as lesson plans, rather, they provide sketches which illustrate how teachers can scaffold children's learning towards the development of big ideas. It is not expected that teachers will teach all the activities, but rather choose to integrate ones which fit best with their curriculum.

Models of good practice

The *models of good practice* are based on a three-stage framework for managing children's science learning which is presented in Loxley et al. (2018). In this book, the framework has been adapted to topic-based learning and used to structure the way children work towards understanding the big ideas. The following provides an overview of the three stages:

1. Exploring children's ideas

Learning starts in the first stage by exploring children's ideas. Children are provided with opportunities to work together and share ideas to complete tasks related to the topic. Working collaboratively, children learn from each other, raise questions, and discover answers through enquiry activities. This stage provides opportunities for formative assessment and identification of misconceptions.

2. Working on scientific understanding

The second stage involves working on scientific understanding that underpins the big idea. This includes providing children with access to the language they need to talk about and mentally engage with the scientific view. For example, in Chapter 3, children are introduced to processes such as evaporation and condensation which underpin the water cycle. They also explore how differences in air pressure create the movement of air in the atmosphere, which we experience as wind. Introducing scientific ideas at this stage provides children with an alternative way of seeing the world, which can help them make sense of the big idea. Loxley et al. (2018) refer to this stage of children's learning as the 're-describing stage' to emphasise the role figurative language plays in helping children to re-think their ideas, and to consequently persuade them to adopt the scientific view as their own.

3. The bigger picture

The third stage provides opportunities for children to explore the bigger picture by using and developing their understanding of the big ideas in other contexts, beyond those explored in the first two stages. For example, in Chapter 6, the focus of the children's learning moves from the impact of the crisis on people's lives in the UK to communities in Eastern Australia which are prone to wildfires. Children then go on to examine the impact of the crisis on some of the world's poorest people, and also explore possible solutions to a human-animal conflict problem.

Indicators of good practice

How children learn is important. The quality of children's learning depends on the nature of the learning opportunities we provide for them. Wynne Harlen's report, *Working with Big Ideas in Science Education*, explores the types of activities and ways of working that help children develop their understanding of big ideas. The report suggests that indicators of good practice are likely to include children having opportunities to:

- understand the purpose of their activities;
- explore new objects or phenomena informally and 'play with ideas' as a preliminary to more structured investigation;
- make links between new and previous experience;
- work collaboratively with others, communicating their own ideas and considering others' ideas;
- present evidence to support their arguments;
- engage in discussions in defence of their ideas and their explanations;
- apply their learning in real-life contexts;
- reflect self-critically about the processes and outcomes of their inquiries.

Research shows that children learn best by sharing ideas and working collaboratively towards common goals in contexts which are familiar and meaningful. The role of the teacher is that of an active participant who guides and assists the children's learning. As the expert, the teacher takes a central role by organising learning tasks, modelling and demonstrating good practice, and helping children to think, talk, and act in ways which support effective learning (Loxley et al., 2018).

Strategies for promoting good practice

Enquiry (including research using information sources)

Enquiry is the cornerstone of science learning through which children develop scientific skills and knowledge. Enquiries start naturally with questions which set children off on a collaborative quest for knowledge to find an answer. Children add to the richness of the quest by speculating about possible solutions and acting to collect evidence in support of their ideas. The plot unfolds when children present their findings and engage in discussion in defence of their ideas. Through whole-class discussion, a negotiated solution is reached and the enquiry brought to a satisfactory resolution. Reflecting on the outcomes of enquiries also provides opportunities for children to voice their opinions and feelings about the value of what they have learnt and what they need to do next in their quest for knowledge.

Story-telling and role-play

Story-telling and role-play enable children to practise using new ideas to guide the way they think and speak in meaningful contexts. Rather than just recounting facts, story-telling and role-play enable children to recognise the value of the new ideas with regard to understanding the world in which they live. It is the link between speaking, listening, thinking, and learning which makes spoken language so important. We can provide children with fascinating experiences of the natural and made world and excellent resources to explore it. But, unless we guide the way they use language to make sense of their experiences, their learning will be diminished and their understanding less secure.

Effective talk

Effective talk enables children to share their thinking and to collaborate so that by working in a group, each child does better than they could have done alone. It is the teacher's job to model and guide the way children interact with each other, to ensure effective science learning. Classes benefit from devising a set of ground rules which help the children remember that talk is a crucial part of science learning. The following rules have been shown to promote effective talk and help children work collaboratively:

- Listen attentively.
- Include everyone in the discussion.
- Ask questions.
- Share relevant information openly.
- Challenge one another's ideas and opinions with respect.
- Ask for and give reasons for ideas.
- Seek to reach agreement before proceeding.
- Support one another during subsequent whole-class discussion.

(Loxley et al., 2018)

Talking points

Talking points is a strategy which can be used to guide group discussion. It is a resource for effective talk developed by Lyn Dawes (2012). Talking points provide starting points for discussion. For example, a talking point could be a simple statement about how clouds are formed, such as: *Water from the sea is used to make clouds*. Groups discuss the idea and together try to decide whether they agree or disagree with the statement, or whether they are unsure. Each member of a group is encouraged to contribute and justify their point of view, and in this way the group works towards an agreed response. Subsequent whole-class discussion orchestrated by the teacher helps everyone to consider a range of views, share their thinking, establish areas of uncertainty for further work, and generally develop their vocabulary and ideas (Loxley et al., 2018).

Publishing

Don't bury children's ideas in their notebooks. Good ideas should not be hidden away and forgotten; they should be published so other people can enjoy them.

> When writing has a purpose, the writer discovers all kinds of important stuff to do with what to write, why write, how write and much more. So, to my mind, we should reconfigure, reframe and reinvent 'writing in schools'. We should think of schools as publishing-performing houses for the exposure and circulation of writing – writing by anyone who works in a school community – pupils, teachers, non-teaching staff – and beyond: parents, grandparents, carers, assistants and so on.
>
> (Michael Rosen, accessed 08/2019 online)

Science publishing in primary schools can be part of a wide genre of writing such as poetry, drama, short stories, music reviews, news articles, book reviews, film reviews, sport reviews, and so on. The climate crisis provides children with lots of interesting and important topics to write about. Publishing for an audience requires children to use their own 'voices' to describe the key ideas, and enables them to experience the satisfaction that authors get from sharing their views with others.

Where to publish are decisions schools have to make in accordance with their e-safety policy. There is a wide choice of blogging platforms, including *Quadblogging*, which links schools in different parts of the world together in fours so that children have a guaranteed audience for their blogs. Collaborating with other schools can be very exciting, and can open children's minds to new ideas and new ways of seeing the world. How to prepare blogs for publication is another matter which needs consideration. To a certain extent, the content of the blogs will need to be edited. How this is done is, again, a matter for individual schools. However, the editing process can provide opportunities for children to re-think their ideas in ways which help them deepen their understanding. Blogs are not the only way children can publish their ideas. Use newsletters, school magazines, science days, school-based science conferences, designated pages on the school website, and so on.

Formative assessment

Formative assessment is an integral part of good practice. It is a continuous process in which information about children's ideas and capabilities is used to help move their learning forward towards the development of bigger ideas.

Opportunities for formative assessment arise whenever children engage in discussion about key ideas. Well-judged questions enable teachers to probe children's thinking and assess their understanding. Talking points can be useful for assessment, as the process of explaining their thinking lays bare the limitations of the children's ideas. Misconceptions can be identified and addressed as part of group or whole-class discussions. Talking points also provide opportunities for peer and self-assessment. Working in small groups allows children to compare and evaluate ideas, and enables them to identify weaknesses in their own understanding.

Other opportunities for formative assessment are provided when children engage in solving puzzles, scientific enquiry, modelling through drama, story-telling, publishing, and describing their ideas through drawings. Listening to children's talk, challenging their ideas, and probing the reasons for their thinking enables teachers to identify their learning needs, and assess their understanding of the key ideas.

Health and safety

There are a number of activities in the following chapters which involve learning outdoors. Outdoor learning presents different risks than those presented in the classroom, and children must be supervised even for short activities within the school grounds. All schools have a policy for the safe conduct of outdoor learning, and many schools have a designated member of staff responsible for ensuring that all visits comply with this policy. It is essential that a risk assessment is carried out and a record kept which can be used to inform subsequent visits. However, each visit should have its own up-to-date risk assessment.

The ASE publication *Be Safe!* (2011) provides extensive guidance on health and safety matters. When planning activities outlined in this book, refer to the relevant ASE *Safety Codes* for guidance. The ASE have published safety codes for:

- Using electrical equipment (p29)
- Studies out of the classroom (p12)
- Heating and burning (p32)
- Food hygiene (p15)
- Making things (p23)
- Gardening (p14)
- Using plants (p18).

As well as safeguarding the wellbeing of the children, activities should also be designed to take care of the plants and animals being studied.

Further reading

- Harlen, W. (ed) (2015) *Working with Big Ideas of Science Education*, published online by IAP.
- Harlen, W. (ed) (2010) *Principles and Big Ideas of Science Education*, published online by IAP.
- Loxley, P., Dawes, L., Nicholls, L., and Dore, B. (2018) *Teaching Primary Science: Promoting Enjoyment and Developing Understanding*. London: Routledge.

Websites

- Big ideas of science education www.ase.org.uk/bigideas
- Climate change: Schools failing us, say pupils – BBC News
- Extensive List of Credible Websites, Newspapers, Journals (scribbr.com)
- If children are to live with the climate crisis, we must green the curriculum | Meryl Batchelder | The Guardian
- Michael Rosen on blogging: https://michaelrosenblog.blogspot.com/2012/07/blogging-for-schools-writing-for.html
- Primary Science Teachers Trust website: https://pstt.org.uk/resources/curriculum-materials/assessment
- Quadblogging: http://quadblogging.net/
- The national curriculum barely mentions the climate crisis. Children deserve better | Fiona Harvey | The Guardian

CHAPTER 2
LISTENING TO THE SCIENCE

Climate crisis: 11,000 scientists warn of untold suffering

This startling headline appeared in an article published by the Guardian newspaper in November 2019. The article reported on a statement in the journal BioScience in which dozens of scientists collaborated to send a message about the dangers of climate change:

> Climate change has arrived and is accelerating faster than many scientists expected. It is more severe than anticipated, threatening natural ecosystems and the fate of humanity. Researchers say they have a moral obligation to clearly warn humanity of any catastrophic threat and tell it like it is. Clearly and unequivocally planet Earth is facing a climate emergency.

A further 11,000 scientists from 153 nations endorsed the statement, warning that climate change will bring untold suffering for large populations of people around the world and the mass extinction of wildlife.

Climate change refers to a large-scale long-term change in the Earth's weather patterns and average temperatures. The scientific evidence for climate change due to increasing carbon dioxide levels in the atmosphere is compelling. If global emissions continue at their current rate, it is possible by the end of the century human activity will have caused the average surface temperature of the planet to rise to more than 4°C higher than its natural level. According to the Met Office, this level of global warming would create adverse effects on the planet which are irreversible and self-reinforcing, and would have serious detrimental effects on nature and on human populations.

Net zero by 2050

In 2015, governments from around the world met in Paris to agree on actions they could take to mitigate the climate crisis. They agreed to substantially reduce greenhouse gas emissions to limit the global temperature rise this century to below 2°C, with a target figure of 1.5°C below pre-industrial levels. They also agreed to review their commitments every five years, to provide funds to developing countries to mitigate climate change, and to help them adapt to climate impacts.

To have at least a 50% chance of achieving the 1.5°C target, scientists believe that current global emissions must be cut by half by 2030, and half again by 2040, and to net zero by 2050 at the latest. To achieve net zero emissions, the world needs to drastically cut its emissions to levels which can be balanced by schemes which remove equivalent

DOI: 10.4324/9781003166276-2

Figure 2.1 Counting the cost of the climate crisis

amounts of greenhouse gases from the air. Achieving net zero by 2050 would require major changes to the way we live and work. These are explored in detail in later chapters.

Time is running out

The Intergovernmental Panel on Climate Change (IPCC) is the United Nations body for assessing the science related to climate change. The IPCC was formed to provide governments and other policymakers with ongoing scientific assessments on climate change, including its implications and potential future risks. In addition, the IPCC provides advice about actions that can be taken to mitigate the impact of the climate crisis.

A report published in August 2021 by the IPCC warned that time was running out to achieve the goals of the 2015 Paris Agreement. Scientists involved in the report warned that limiting warming to 1.5°C or even 2°C will be beyond reach unless there are immediate, rapid, and large-scale reductions in carbon dioxide and other greenhouse gas emissions. The report shows that greenhouse gases from human activities are responsible for close to 1.1°C of warming since 1850–1900, and find that global warming will reach or exceed 1.5°C in the next 20 years.

The report projects that in the coming decades climate changes will increase in all regions. For 1.5°C of global warming, there will be increasing heatwaves, longer warm seasons, and shorter cold seasons. At 2°C of global warming, heat extremes would often reach levels which endanger people's health and have damaging impacts on agriculture.

Figure 2.2 Global temperatures on the rise

As I write, much of Europe and North America are experiencing record high temperatures, and devastating wildfires are wiping out enormous areas of forest and destroying people's homes.

The following extract is taken from a keynote speech made by the IPCC Chair, Hoesung Lee. The speech provides an up-to-date context for this book, as it clearly points out the way forward towards a sustainable future after the Covid-19 pandemic.

> This year due to Covid-19 the world has seen a tremendous drop in CO2 emissions. . . . But there are already signs that emissions are rebounding as economies reopen. We recall that the economic recovery following the 2008 global financial crisis brought with it the biggest jump in emissions in history. The world cannot afford to repeat that history, because there is no time to lose. We need a sharp structural decline of greenhouse gas emissions. This requires a dramatic acceleration in the transitions to clean, sustainable energy that are already underway in many countries and industries. This will be a new opportunity presented to the financial sectors. The good news is we already have affordable, reliable technologies that can put the peak in global emissions behind us and start the drive down to net zero. Deployed quickly and on a major scale, the clean energy technologies we have now can bring about the decline in energy-related emissions that would put the world on track for the climate goals. The governments around the world now pursue to counter the impacts of the Covid-19. It offers a unique momentum to shift the investment from the traditional greenhouse gas intensive technologies to the technologies for sustainable future.
>
> (IPCC Chair Hoesung Lee, September 2020)

Conference of the Parties (COP)

UN climate change conferences, called Conference of the Parties (COP), are regular events which bring together heads of state, climate experts, and campaigners to agree on coordinated action to tackle climate change. The twenty-sixth conference (COP 26) was held in Glasgow (UK) in November 2021.

With global emissions still rising, COP 26 was supposed to be a landmark conference at which nations could unambiguously commit themselves to achieving net zero emissions by 2050, and keep 1.5°C of warming within reach. Other goals of the conference included:

- To encourage countries to adapt to the effects of climate change to protect communities and natural habitats
- To make available at least $100bn (£74bn) in climate finance per year to help developing countries adapt to climate change
- To encourage collaboration between governments, businesses, and civil society in order to accelerate climate action, and to achieve the goals set out in the Paris Agreement

According to many scientists, the outcomes of the conference were disappointing, with pledges on cutting emissions falling well short of those required. For example, a pledge to 'phase down' the use of 'unabated' coal power stations was agreed. However, no timescale for this to happen was produced, leaving the biggest polluters, such as India and China, uncommitted to any serious action. Instead, it was agreed that there was an urgent need to negotiate more ambitious cuts to greenhouse gas emissions at the conference in Egypt in 2022. On a more optimistic note, the final text recognised the important role that indigenous peoples, local communities, youth, children, local and regional governments, and other stakeholders play in tackling the climate crisis.

Despite the pledges made in the conference, scientists warn that the world is still nowhere near its goal on limiting global temperature rise to 1.5°C, and more likely we are heading for 2.4°C of warming by 2100. According to the research group Climate Action Tracker (CAT), COP26 has a massive credibility gap, due to many countries pledging more than they are likely to achieve in reality. In spite of the promises made at COP26, CAT concludes that, by 2030, greenhouse gas emissions will be twice as high as they need to be to limit warming to below 1.5°C. Climate activist Greta Thunberg accused the conference of green-washing and called for real climate action, not just more blah! blah! blah!

The Earthshot Prize

It is not only governments that need to take action to tackle the climate crisis. Non-government organisations (NGOs) around the world are making important contributions, including charities such as WaterAid, Practical Action, and many more.

An initiative was launched in October 2021 by The Royal Foundation of The Duke and Duchess of Cambridge, called the Earthshot Prize. The purpose of the prize is to provide an incentive for people to take action that can help repair our planet over the next ten years. In the words of Prince William, The Duke of Cambridge:

The Earth is at a tipping point and we face a stark choice: either we continue as we are and irreparably damage our planet, or we remember our unique power as human beings and our continual ability to lead, innovate and problem-solve. People can achieve great things. The next ten years present us with one of our greatest tests – a decade of action to repair the Earth.

The Earthshot Prize takes its inspiration from President John F. Kennedy's Moonshot initiative which united millions of people around the goal of putting a man on the Moon. The goals for the Earthshot Prize involve five ambitious challenges or 'Earthshots' to be achieved by 2030, which will help repair the planet and improve life for us all. The five Earthshot challenges and the inaugural winners in 2021 were:

1. *Protect and restore nature*: The government of Costa Rica pioneered a project which paid locals to protect forests, plant trees, and restore natural ecosystems. The results were extraordinary, resulting in forests doubling in size and a boom in ecotourism.
2. *Clean our air:* The Indian company Takachar found a solution to air pollution caused by agricultural waste.
3. *Revive our oceans:* Coral Vita, a scheme in the Bahamas, grow coral on land before replanting it in the ocean.
4. *Fix our climate:* AEM electrolyser, an international project involving Thai, German, and Italian researchers which has come up with clean hydrogen-fuel technology providing fuel for cars, planes, and heating.
5. *Build a waste-free world:* The city of Milan set up hubs across the city to collect waste food from supermarkets before donating it to charities. The scheme has dramatically cut waste while tackling hunger.

Each of the winners received one million pounds to support and develop their project.

Figure 2.3 Activists call for more climate action

Climate change activists

Although many governments have set targets to reduce climate emissions, many activists believe that not enough is being done to achieve those targets.

> I have seen too much destruction and death from the floods. My country has felt too much heartache. For the next five years, I want to see not just targets that actually align with the Paris agreement, but concrete plans on how to achieve those targets.
>
> Mitzi Jonelle Tan (Manila, Philippines)

Many of the climate activists around the world are too young to vote, and instead have taken to social media to get their views heard. Greta Thunberg is probably the most well-known young activist with over 8 million followers on Instagram. Greta is just one of many young activists who are determined that governments should do a lot more to combat climate change.

Young activists have shown that you do not need to be rich or famous to make a difference. None of us can change the world in one stroke, but we can all do things that collectively lead to a less polluted and safer world. For example, young UK activists Ella and Caitlin McEwan petitioned fast-food restaurants to stop putting plastic toys in kids' meals. As a result, Burger King said it would remove the toys, and McDonald's promised to give customers the choice of a toy or fruit. Kenyan activist Lesein Mutunei combines his love of football with his desire to combat the climate crisis by planting a tree for every goal he scores. Small acts like this can make a difference, by encouraging other young people to take action to improve the environment.

All around the world, young people have been demanding greater action from governments to combat the climate crisis. Famously, they have taken part in the global Future for Friday climate strikes and have participated at international conferences, such as the UN's Youth Climate Summit in New York. In November 2020, young activists from 140 countries organised a huge international virtual conference. The conference coincided with the 5th anniversary of the 2015 Paris Agreement. Policies derived from the conference called for climate education at every level of formal education, tougher laws against the destruction of wildlife and ecosystems, stronger regulation of air quality, and a commitment to limiting global warming to below 1.5°C.

Prior to COP 26, young people from around the world held their own climate change conference, called the Conference of Youth (COY 16). The overarching demand which emerged from the conference was the youth should be actively and meaningfully included in all decision-making processes concerning which actions to take to tackle climate change, and also play a role to ensure their implementation. Top of the list of the key demands is that all actions taken by national governments should be aligned with the science.

Information sources

- Climate change: 7 young climate activists from around the world – CBBC Newsround
- COP26 Goals – UN Climate Change Conference (COP26) at the SEC – Glasgow 2021 (ukcop26.org)

- COP26: World on track for 2.4°C warming despite climate summit – report – BBC News
- Earthshot Prize
- Global youth statement (ukcoy16.org)
- IPCC – Intergovernmental Panel on Climate Change
- 'Mock Cop26' activists vote on treaty ahead of 2021 climate summit | Climate change | The Guardian
- Only 11 Years Left to Prevent Irreversible Damage from Climate Change, Speakers Warn during General Assembly High-Level Meeting | Meetings Coverage and Press Releases (un.org)
- Opinion: This Is the World Being Left to Us by Adults – Greta Thunberg, Adriana Calderón, Farzana Faruk Jhumu, and Eric Njuguna via The New York Times | Coyote Gulch
- Paris climate agreement 5th anniversary: 5 youth activists share their hopes for what's next – Vox
- The Paris Agreement | United Nations
- What are the goals of COP26? Purpose of Glasgow climate change conference – and how it relates to Paris Agreement and UN Framework | The Scotsman

CHAPTER 3

WEATHER

Big idea: *Processes that occur on the Earth's surface and in its atmosphere combine to shape its weather and its climate.*

This chapter focuses on developing children's understanding of the causes of different types of weather, and also explores the history of weather forecasting. The first part of the chapter sets out subject knowledge for teachers to help them support children's learning towards the big idea. Part 2 of the chapter sets out models of good practice which provide ideas and activities which teachers can use to organise children's learning.

The subject knowledge topics include:

- The atmosphere
- Solar energy
- Water cycle
- Types of weather
- Weather forecasts

Part 1: Subject knowledge

The atmosphere

We live at the bottom of a sea of air, called the atmosphere. The atmosphere is mainly made from nitrogen (78%) and oxygen (21%), with small amounts of carbon dioxide (0.04%) and other gases. The processes that shape the weather mostly occur in the troposphere, which is the layer of air closest to Earth's surface. This is where the air is the thickest (most dense) and where most of the weather events occur. Because the air is thicker, the air pressure is greater closer to the Earth and gradually gets less as we go higher.

Figure 3.1 Clouds form in the troposphere

Solar energy

At any given time, there is a massive 16,300 kW of solar energy arriving on Earth for every person in the world. According to Berners-Lee (2019), the Sun provides enough energy for each of us to bring an Olympic swimming pool to a boil every day. Most of the Sun's energy lands in the sea where it is mainly out of our reach and, not being available to heat swimming pools, the Earth uses it to power the processes that shape our weather and our climate.

What is the weather like where you are today? If children look out the window, they are able to describe the weather. Is it raining? Is it sunny? Is it foggy? Is it warm or cold out there? Maybe it's dry but a little windy, or maybe there is a gale blowing. Whatever the weather is like today, the Sun in some way is responsible.

Water cycle

The most-talked-about weather event is rain. Before we leave the house, we all want to know whether it will rain so that we can choose suitable clothes. It rains because the water in lakes, seas, oceans, and rivers is involved in a constant cycle of heating, evaporation, convection, cooling, condensation, and precipitation. Heat energy from the Sun evaporates the water turning the liquid into a gas (water vapour) which rises (convection) into the atmosphere. Plants, such as trees, also release water vapour into the atmosphere through their leaves. Plants, of course, rely on the Sun's energy to grow.

As the water vapour rises in the atmosphere it cools and condenses from a gas into liquid water droplets to form clouds. Within the clouds the water droplets merge together

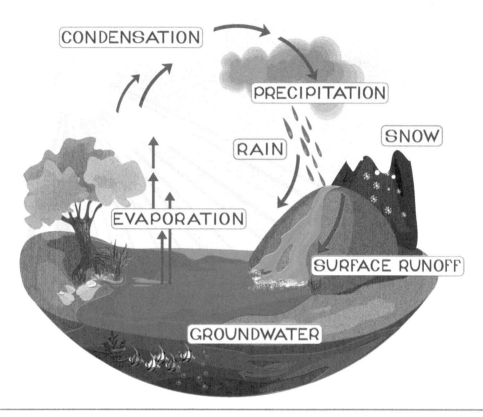

Figure 3.2 Water cycle

to form larger ones, which may become heavy enough to fall back down to Earth as rain (precipitation). In low temperatures, water droplets in clouds can freeze creating ice crystals, which fall to the ground as snow or hail.

When it reaches the Earth's surface, the rainwater may flow back into lakes, seas, oceans, and rivers, or it may soak into the ground. Water that soaks into the ground may slowly find its way into a river, or be absorbed by the roots of plants to help them grow. Back on the Earth's surface, the water is ready to be recycled again. The water cycle provides an example of how some materials, such as water, change state when heated or cooled.

Types of weather

Foggy weather

Foggy weather is a clear sign that winter is on the way. Fog is created when the air close to the ground becomes saturated with water vapour, which condenses to form tiny water droplets suspended in the air.

Humidity is a measure of the water vapour in the air. It measures how close the air is to being saturated with water vapour. For example, 100% humidity tells us that the air is saturated and cannot hold any more water vapour. Once the air is saturated, the vapour condenses into water droplets, creating mist (fog) and rain. The temperature of the air affects the amount of water vapour it can hold. Less water vapour is needed to saturate the air at lower temperatures, and hence fog is more likely to form in autumn and winter than the warmer months. In the UK, the average humidity in autumn is 87%, compared with 79% in the summer months. The higher the humidity, the more uncomfortable the air makes us feel because it affects our body's cooling system by preventing sweat evaporating from our skin. Evaporation of sweat causes our skin to cool down, which happens more efficiently when we are surrounded by drier air.

Windy weather

Windy weather is caused by differences in air pressure. Winds are created when hot air expands and rises, leaving behind a space containing low-pressure air into which the surrounding high-pressure air can move. The movement of air from areas of high pressure to areas of lower pressure creates the wind. On weather maps, isobars are lines that join places of equal pressure. By identifying areas of low and high pressure, isobars enable the direction and the strength of the wind to be predicted. The closer together the isobars, the greater the difference in pressure and the stronger the wind.

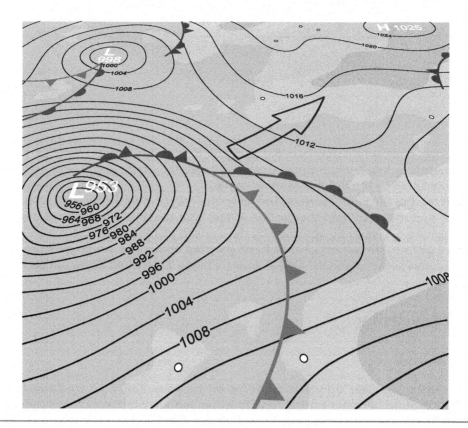

Figure 3.3 Weather map

The wind is always named from the direction from which it blows. For example, a north wind is a wind which blows from the north to the south. In the UK, north winds often bring cold weather as they originate from the vast area of ice and snow in the Arctic. Winds from the west tend to be warmer and wetter than those from the north. Westerly winds can travel over a large area of the Atlantic Ocean where they pick up lots of moisture, often resulting in rainy weather.

Wind speed is measured using an instrument called an anemometer, and is often measured in nautical units called knots. One knot is approximately equal to 1.9 km per hour. Wind speeds vary from a light breeze of 4–6 knots (6–11 kph) to hurricane speed, which can be greater than 64 knots, which is 118 km per hour.

Thunderstorms

Thunderstorms can be both exciting and terrifying, especially when they involve spectacular lightning strikes. Thunderstorms are created when warm air containing large amounts of water vapour is trapped beneath clouds containing much colder water droplets. As the warmer air rises, it combines with the much colder water droplets in the clouds. Water vapour in the air quickly cools and condenses to form huge unstable cumulonimbus clouds. Typically, these giant storm clouds form very quickly, often in less than an hour.

As warm air continues to rise water droplets get bigger and colder, and freeze to create ice crystals (hail) which eventually fall back down to the bottom of the cloud. The

Figure 3.4 Lightning strike

movement of ice crystals within the cloud creates static electricity due to the ice crystals rubbing against each other. Consequently, a large negative charge forms at the base of the cloud, while a large positive charge is created near the top. The charging of a thunder cloud can be compared to charging a plastic rod by rubbing it with a duster. When rubbed against each other the rod becomes negatively charged, while the cloth becomes positively charged.

Lightning is a large electric spark which travels from the negatively charged base of a thundercloud down to the ground. Lightning also occurs between clouds when negative charges in a cloud are attracted to the positive charges in another cloud. Lightning is caused by negatively charged electrons moving from one place to another. Electrons cannot be seen, but when they are moving extremely fast, the air around them glows, causing the lightning flash. The actual streak of lightning is the path the electrons follow when they move.

Hurricanes

Hurricanes can be devastating, causing huge amounts of damage and substantial loss of life. Hurricane Katrina hit the USA in 2005, causing over 1800 deaths and $125 billion in damage.

Going back in history, we can find even deadlier hurricanes. In 1780, the Great Hurricane smashed into the region of Lesser Antilles, killing around 22,000 people. Wind speeds were estimated to exceed 320 km/h.

Figure 3.5 Eye of a hurricane

Hurricanes are a swirling mass of wind, rain, thunder, and chaos. They grow from thunderclouds which begin to rotate and draw up huge amounts of energy and water vapour from the warm ocean. The eye is a calm region at the centre of the hurricane, which can be 30 to 65 kilometres (20 to 40 miles) wide. Inside the eye it is possible to see the blue sky or the starry night above. The eye is surrounded by the eyewall, which is typically 16 kilometres (10 miles) thick. This is where all the most severe weather occurs, including intense rain, thunderstorms, and extremely high winds. A category five hurricane has wind speeds that exceed 252 km/h (157 m/hr). Surrounding the eyewall are the rain bands, which can stretch hundreds of miles from the centre to give the storm its size. In these regions, the wind and rain come in heavy bursts.

Scientists believe that it is likely hurricanes will become more frequent and more intense as the oceans become warmer. Already there is evidence for this, with the 2020 Atlantic hurricane season being the most active on record.

Weather forecasts

Children may be fascinated to know that the man who invented the weather forecast was none other than Admiral Robert FitzRoy. He was the same Robert FitzRoy who was captain of the HMS Beagle, on which Charles Darwin sailed around the world. Today, FitzRoy is chiefly remembered for the part he played in Darwin's famous expedition but, in his own time, he was more famous for his daily weather forecasts.

Weather forecasts did not exist in 1854 when FitzRoy established what later would be called the Met Office. Before then, people relied on 'weather wisdom' to decide when it was best to do their outdoor jobs. For example, farmers watched out for signs in nature to decide the best time to plant crops. They observed the appearance of clouds or the behaviour of animals to help them decide the coming weather. Through the years, people developed catchy sayings as a way of passing their 'weather wisdom' on to the next generation, such as:

- *When the swallows fly high, the weather will be dry.*
- *When sheep collect and huddle, tomorrow will become a puddle.*
- *Bats flying late in the evening foretell a fine next day.*
- *St. Swithin's Day if thou dost rain, for 40 days it will remain.*
- *If the ash leafs out before the oak, expect a wet season.*
- *February thunder brings a May frost.*

In the mid-19th century, science and technology were all the rage in Victorian Britain, and scientists found it embarrassing that people believed a bat or a swallow was able to detect a coming storm before they could. At this time, scientists understood storms and were able to formulate weather charts showing centres of low and high air pressure. However, they could not make accurate national weather forecasts because they were not able to collect real-time data from around the country.

FitzRoy's achievement was to use the newly invented electric telegraph system to collect real-time weather data from coastal areas around Britain. He used the data to forecast storms and other weather events two days in advance, which he published in several newspapers, including the Times.

The Times weather forecast for 1 August 1861

The temperature in London was to be 62F (16.7C), clear with a south-westerly wind. The temperature in Liverpool was to be 61F, very cloudy with a light south-westerly wind. It was to be overcast in Nairn, Portsmouth and Dover with the latter predicted to hit a pleasant 70F, the same as Lisbon.

BBC News online

FitzRoy's forecasts weren't always accurate and, on many occasions, he faced criticism and mockery. A typical complaint was made in the Cork Examiner:

Yesterday, at two o'clock, we received by telegraph Admiral FitzRoy's signal of a southerly gale. The gallant meteorologist might have sent it by post, as the gale had commenced the day before and concluded fully twelve hours before the receipt of the warning.

BBC News online

Predicting the weather is a complex process, and it is no surprise that FitzRoy's forecasts were often inaccurate. Today's forecasters have the help of a global communication system, with satellites orbiting the Earth and supercomputers to work out the weather, and they still don't get it right all the time. FitzRoy was a pioneer at the start of a very long journey, one that continues today in the Met Office.

Part 2: Working towards the big idea

This part provides ideas and activities which enable children to work towards understanding the big idea within a framework of good practice. Learning starts by exploring and building on children's experiences of extreme weather events, such as thunderstorms and hurricanes. Opportunities are provided to observe and record the weather, and to post their data on the Met Office Weather Observation website. Activities then focus on helping children work on their scientific understanding of the processes which shape the weather, including evaporation, condensation, and how differences in air pressure cause the wind. Looking at the bigger picture, children explore the history and accuracy of weather forecasting, and are given the opportunity to present their own forecast. The ideas presented are consistent with primary science and geography programmes of study.

Children have opportunities to develop and use the following science and design technology skills:

- Work collaboratively towards common goals.
- Use different types of scientific enquiries, including data gathering and fair testing.
- Research using secondary sources.
- Generate, develop, model, and communicate ideas through discussion, sketches, and prototypes.
- Communicate outcomes of their research and enquiry in different ways.
- Apply their learning in real-life contexts.

Health and safety

Follow the health and safety guidelines in the ASE Publication *Be Safe!* when planning the condensation activity (Heating and burning p31).

Exploring children's ideas

Colour-coding the atmosphere

Start this topic with an image of the different layers in the atmosphere. Talk about its structure and point out that most weather events occur in the troposphere. Challenge children to use watercolours to interpret the complexity of the atmosphere, by painting an image in which the gases are colour-coded. For example, nitrogen could be blue, oxygen red, carbon dioxide yellow, and so on. They use the colours to create an imaginative representation of the atmosphere, bearing in mind how the air gets thinner at higher altitudes. Children can use information sources to discover where the atmosphere ends and space begins. They can add objects such as birds, clouds, exploding volcanoes, aeroplanes, satellites, The International Space Station, space rockets, and other dynamic objects to create a visual narrative. Talk together about their paintings, and ask them to justify where they have placed their objects in their representations.

Research! Hurricanes

Indulge in the great British pastime of talking about the weather. To get children interested, talk about the exciting stuff first. Talk about thunderstorms and hurricanes. Show children video clips of hurricanes. Listen to children's experiences of thunderstorms, and perhaps even a hurricane! Ask children whether they think thunderstorms and hurricanes are connected? Talk about how hurricanes grow from thunderstorms out in the ocean, and how they begin to rotate and draw up huge amounts of energy and water vapour from the warm ocean. Lots of examples of hurricanes may be found on the National Geographic website.

Groups use information sources to research the causes, structure, and destructive power of hurricanes. People who have experienced a hurricane know the devastation they can cause, flattening homes, ripping up trees, and creating huge storm surges. In fact, according to NASA, during its lifecycle a hurricane can expend as much energy as 10,000 nuclear bombs. Children present their findings in the form of a documentary using images and videos of real events taken from the web to illustrate their presentations. Each group should include three facts chosen to fascinate their audience.

Model! Tornadoes in a jar

Tornadoes form over land and are much smaller than hurricanes. While a hurricane may last for days or even weeks, tornadoes normally last a few minutes. It is easy to model a

Figure 3.6 Destructive power of a hurricane

Figure 3.7 Tornado

Figure 3.8 Girls with static hair

tornado in a jar. All you need is a clear jam jar or see-through container with a screw-on lid. Fill the container with water and add a few drops of washing-up liquid, together with a few drops of food colouring. Then, screw the lid back on. Swirl the container around and around, and then stop. Inside you should see a mini tornado, which will slowly disappear as it reaches the top of the container. Children can explore the effects on the shape of the tornado of swirling the jar at different speeds and changing the temperature of the water.

Model! Thunderclouds

Show children video clips of thunder and lightning. Talk about how static electricity builds up at the top and bottom of the thundercloud, and how this produces lightning. Borrow a Van der Graaf Generator from the local secondary school and use it to simulate lightning. Children can produce static electricity by blowing up a balloon and rubbing it against their hair. Once the balloon is charged, children use the electric force field on it to pick up small bits of paper, rice grains, and to roll an empty aluminium can along the desk. What other materials are attracted to the balloon? Talk about how parts of a thundercloud are charged when ice and water particles in the cloud rub against each other, just like rubbing a balloon.

Design! Weather symbols

Talk together about the different kinds of weather. Listen to their ideas and list what children think are the most essential terms. Together, identify terms such as rain, wind, fog, sunshine, cloud, snow, hail, thunder, lightning, and so on. Children use their imaginations to design symbols to depict different weather events, making them more creative and fun than those often seen on national weather charts.

Design! Met Office weather reports

To learn to talk about the weather in scientific ways, children can explore the way the BBC and Met Office describe the weather in their weather apps. Forecasts often start with a brief overview, such as: *light cloud and moderate breeze* or *sunny intervals and gentle breeze* to help the public visualise what the weather will be like at particular times of the day. This brief description is followed by data concerning humidity, air pressure, temperature, probability of rain, and wind speed.

The following example was taken from a BBC weather forecast for a winter's day in Salisbury (UK).

1400: Light rain and a moderate breeze

- Humidity: 87%
- Visibility: Good
- Pressure: 1019 mb
- Temperature feels like 4°C
- High chance of precipitation: 88%
- A moderate breeze from the northeast: 17 knots

Ask the children what they understand by each part of the forecast. Could the forecast be made more child-friendly? Is all the data necessary? Ask children to interpret and redesign the forecast so it is more interesting and easier to understand.

Weather watchers

To become weather watchers, children will need equipment, such as simple rainfall gauges, thermometers, anemometers, weather vanes, and barometers. Groups use their instruments to record the weather each day. They can share their weather observations on the Met Office Weather Observation Website (WOW). The Met Office uses its WOW website to coordinate the growth of the weather-observing community, and to enable schools to compare their weather observations with the closest Met Office Station and other sites across the world. Schools that publish their results on WOW can also compare their data with other schools in the UK and in other parts of the world.

Explore! Clouds

Clouds are brilliant things to explore, both aesthetically and scientifically. Allow a time each week for children to do their observations, which they record using sketches and photographs in a cloud diary. They record what the clouds look like,

Figure 3.9 High altitude clouds
Source: Anna Loxley

whether they are low or high in the sky, and which direction they are moving in. Encourage them to describe the clouds using language such as dark and dense, or light and wispy, and so on. In the classroom, children use the Met Office Clouds website to identify and find out how different types of clouds are formed. Children come together in groups to share their ideas. Display sketches and photographs of different types of clouds.

Paint! Clouds

Children use watercolours to create their own representations of clouds in the sky at different times of the year. Their paintings should depict a weather event, with a focus on the shapes, colour, and texture of the clouds in the sky. For example, they could paint a hailstorm, a thunderstorm, snowy weather, light rain showers, or just a nice sunny day. The paintings should be creative artworks and not scientific illustrations, although they should be based on their own cloud and weather observations. Encourage children to explore the works of Turner and Constable to discover how they paint clouds and different weather events.

Information sources

Websites

- BBC Weather
- Earth Minute Videos | Explore – Climate Change: Vital Signs of the Planet (nasa.gov)
- Make a tornado in a jar – Met Office
- Met Office WOW – Home Page
- How Hurricanes Form | UCAR Center for Science Education
- Hurricane (nationalgeographic.com)
- Hurricane Katrina Historic Storm Surge Video – Gulfport, Mississippi – Bing video
- Hurricanes 101 | National Geographic – Bing video
- Hurricanes release energy of 10,000 nuclear bombs | Global Ideas | DW | 21.09.2017
- Hurricanes: The Greatest Storms on Earth (nasa.gov)
- Hurricanes/Tropical Cyclones | NASA
- Tropical cyclone facts – Met Office
- WWF_KS2_Lesson1_Presentation.pdf

Working on scientific understanding

In this part children work on their understanding of how energy from the Sun powers the processes that shape our weather.

How clouds are created

Use the talking points to get children thinking and sharing ideas.

Talking points: true, false, or not sure?

- Clouds are made of water.
- Clouds are made of smoke from factories.
- Dark clouds are made of dirty water.
- White clouds are full of steam.
- Water from the sea is used to make clouds.
- Heat from the Sun creates clouds.
- Heat from deserts creates clouds.
- Mountains create clouds.

Discuss children's responses to the talking points. Encourage them to justify their ideas. Focus on misconceptions and areas of uncertainty. Talk about evaporation and condensation as the processes which are responsible for the formation of clouds. Use illustrations and animations to explain the water cycle.

Figure 3.10 Super cloud

Model! Water Cycle

Working in large groups, children role-model the water cycle. Choose one of the children to be the narrator. They will need space to role-play evaporation. Use the school hall or playground. Children huddle together in a group to represent a large drop of water, with each one representing a tiny particle of the liquid. Like all liquids water is fluid, meaning that the particles must be free to move within the body of the water. Children can model the fluid nature of the water by moving around within the group. When heated by energy from the Sun, particles become more energetic and move around more vigorously, bumping into each other. The ones moving fastest would fly out of the liquid into the air. The hotter the water the more vigorous the movement, resulting in higher rates of evaporation. Children at the edges 'fly off' first, followed in turn by the other children. Eventually the hall or playground is filled with water vapour, represented by children moving freely in all directions.

Children reverse their model of evaporation to model condensation and the formation of clouds. Start with children moving freely around. As the temperature falls, the children slow down and gravitate together in small groups to form water droplets in a cloud. As the temperature continues to fall, the droplets combine to form one big rain droplet which is too heavy to remain floating in the air. The droplet now falls down to Earth as rain. Talk about how when the air temperatures are low, water droplets in clouds can freeze, creating ice crystals which fall to Earth as snow or hail. Challenge the children to model how water turns into solid ice.

Enquire! Evaporation

Working in groups, children plan investigations to discover how temperature influences rates of evaporation. Focus discussion on controlling variables so their tests are fair. They can extend their enquiry to look at the effects of surface area and wind factors. Children record their results appropriately and draw conclusions about how different conditions affect rates of evaporation. Challenge children to explain their results by reasoning from the evaporation model described earlier. Link this to the work you do on states of matter. More information can be found in Loxley 2018.

Condensation

With the children watching at a safe distance, bring in a thermos of hot water and pour some of it into a bowl. Hold a cold surface, at fridge temperature, over the rising steam to demonstrate condensation. Listen to children's ideas about why steam condenses on the cold surface. What do they think is happening to the water particles? Talk about how the water particles slow down when they get cold and start to clump together again, to form a liquid.

Explore! Wind

To understand the causes of wind, children need to have some understanding of air pressure. Children can experience air pressure by inflating balloons, and feeling the pressure increase as more air is forced inside. Talk together about how the air pressure inside an inflated balloon is greater than the air pressure outside the balloon. When the air inside is released, children can feel it gushing out of the hole. Compare the movement of the air to wind, and point out that air always moves from areas of high pressure to areas of low pressure. Talk about how wind is created in the atmosphere by the movement of air from areas of high pressure to areas of low pressure.

Turn children's learning into a game with the help of a ping pong ball, a balloon, an air pump, and objects to make an obstacle course. The idea is for children to inflate the balloon and control the release of the 'wind' so they can push the ping pong ball around the obstacle course. Encourage children to change the pressure inside the balloon, and observe the effects on the ping pong ball. How does the force of the 'wind' change as the pressure inside the balloon is increased? Does higher pressure create more force on the ball? Talk about how higher air pressure in the atmosphere can create stronger winds. The bigger the difference between the high-pressure air and the low-pressure air, the stronger the wind.

Explore! Air

Working in groups, children use a plastic syringe to explore the properties of air. They start by filling the syringe with air and then try to compress the plunger with a finger over the end of the syringe to stop the air escaping. Ask children to describe what they experience. Can they feel the pressure of the air in the syringe increase the further they push in the plunger? Encourage children to speculate reasons for why air is compressible and springy. Explain that air (and other gases) spread out to fill the container. By pushing in the plunger, the air particles are squashed closer together, which increases the air pressure. When the plunger is released, the air expands and pushes the plunger out. Use this as an example of air moving from higher to lower pressure.

To explore the effect heat has on air pressure, children half-fill a syringe with air and seal the end. Place the barrel of the syringe in a container filled with hot tap water, with the plunger sticking out. Children should see the plunger move out. Challenge them to explain why. Talk about how the heat from the water causes the air inside the plunger to expand.

Model! Air

Children design and build their own models to represent the structure of air. One idea is to partially fill an open basket with different sized or coloured polystyrene balls to represent the different gas particles, and blow air through the basket using a hair dryer. The lighter the balls, the more they will fly about. Point out how the balls represent the air particles moving about rapidly, bouncing off the sides of the container. Talk about the space between the particles, and how the particles could be squashed together to fit into a smaller space. Challenge children to design their own models of a gas and a liquid.

Information sources

Websites

- Atmosphere | National Geographic Society
- Clouds – Met Office
- Earth's Atmospheric Layers | NASA
- How do we measure the weather? – Met Office
- Learn about weather – Met Office
- Our resources for 7–11-year-olds – Met Office
- Understanding weather – Met Office
- Weather for young people – Met Office

Books

- Loxley, P., Dawes, L., Nicholls, L., and Dore, B. (2018) *Teaching Primary Science*. Abingdon: Routledge.
- Loxley, P. (2018) *Practical Ideas for Teaching Primary Science*. Abingdon: Routledge.

The bigger picture

In this part, children learn about the history and nature of weather forecasting. They start by designing and presenting their own weather forecast.

Design! Weather forecasts

Show children video clips of weather reports being presented on the TV. Discuss the key features of the reports.

Focus children's attention on the weather charts and explain that an isobar is a line that joins up areas of equal air pressure. Point out that areas of low pressure are often called depressions, and are associated with rainy conditions. On the other hand, areas of

Figure 3.11 Weather Studio

high pressure often signal more settled weather. Talk together about how the direction and strength of the wind could be predicted from these charts, bearing in mind that the wind always moves from areas of high pressure to low pressure.

Working in groups, children plan to present a weather report designed for their age group. The reports should be based on real and current weather forecasts.

Encourage children to be creative and design their own charts and graphics. When planning their presentations, groups should think about:

1.   The audience – who do they expect to be watching?
2.   A 'top line' that summarises the most striking parts of the forecast
3.   Their main message – what do they think their audience wants to know?
4.   Little bits of information which grab the imagination of the audience
5.   How will they finish the forecast?

More ideas about how to write and present a weather forecast can be found on the BBC School Report: Introduction to Weather Forecasting website. Help children edit their weather forecasts. Groups present and video record their presentations, which can be shared with the rest of the school during an assembly and/or published on the school's preferred social media platform.

Enquire! Accuracy of weather forecast

Groups plan enquiries to test the accuracy of the two-week forecast provided by the BBC Weather app. They start by recording the BBC forecast for each day of the two weeks. They then collect their own data. Each day they record visibility, outside temperature, rainfall, wind strength, and direction. At the end of each week, children share and discuss their results. How accurate were the BBC weather forecasts? Was the first week more accurate than the second one? Can we expect forecasts to be 100% accurate? Encourage children to estimate the accuracy of the forecasts using a scale from 0–100%. Talk about how the atmosphere is vast and complex, and how it is impossible to monitor accurately every process on the Earth's surface and in the atmosphere which contribute to the weather. Point out that just small changes in ocean currents can significantly change the weather.

Research! Blowing in the wind

Satellite technology is used for monitoring weather events throughout the world, and is an important part of weather forecasting. Show children the NASA Earth Minute video entitled 'Blowing in the wind', and talk about how the use of satellites has improved weather and hurricane forecasts. Groups use information sources to explore the different ways NASA and the Met Office use satellites to collect weather data. Each group creates and presents their own minute video to explain what they have discovered.

Survey! How forecasts are used

Discuss how children use weather forecasts. Do weather forecasts help them make choices? Do members of their family find weather forecasts useful? What choices did weather forecasts help them make in the past? How accurate were the forecasts?

Figure 3.12 Great weather for a BBQ!

Children survey family and friends to discover how they make use of the weather forecast. Collate the results of the survey under headings such as choosing clothes, travel, work, gardening, holidays, leisure, sport, barbeques, shopping, and so on.

Working in groups, children explore how industries such as fishing, agriculture, construction, retail, and others rely on the weather forecast. Children imagine they are buyers for a large retail clothing outlet. It is winter and they need to order stock from their manufacturers for their spring collection. Groups start by making predictions about what they think the weather will be like. Do they expect a mild, wet spring, or a dry, hot one? Can they find any information from the Met Office website that will help them make their predictions? How far in advance can the weather be forecast? Is it better to look at trends in the weather from previous years to help them decide? Is spring weather always the same or is it changing? Weather data from previous years can be found on the Met Office website. What other factors do they need to take into account when choosing the spring collection?

Having done their research, groups decide on ten items of clothing which they think will be bestsellers in the spring. Before they can order the clothes from the manufacturers, groups need to persuade the CEO (teacher) and other board members (class members) that they are the right choices for their prestigious spring collection. Children should present the weather data when justifying their choices. How would next year's winter collection differ from the spring choices?

Storytelling! The history of weather forecasting

Working in small groups, children use secondary sources to tell the story of the history of meteorology from the time of the Victorians to the present day. Their narratives should start with the Victorians' love of science and the pioneering work of Admiral Robert FitzRoy. The stories should provide a flavour of the complexity of weather forecasting and provide insights into the work done by the Met Office today.

Information sources

Websites

- How are weather forecasts made? – BBC News
- Met Office and Forecasting Firsts – Met Office
- School Report – Introduction to weather forecasting (bbc.co.uk)
- School Report – Presenting a weather forecast (bbc.co.uk)
- Surface Pressure Charts – Met Office
- The birth of the weather forecast – BBC News
- UK temperature, rainfall, and sunshine time series – Met Office
- Weather forecast for the UK – BBC Weather

CHAPTER 4
CLIMATE

Big idea: *Processes that occur on the Earth's surface and in its atmosphere combine to shape its weather and its climate.*

This chapter focuses on developing children's understanding of climate and the influence seasonal temperatures have on the behaviour of the natural world. The first part of the chapter sets out subject knowledge for teachers to help them support children's learning towards the big idea. Part 2 of the chapter sets out models of good practice which provide ideas and activities that teachers can use to organise children's learning. The ideas presented are consistent with primary science and geography programmes of study.

The subject knowledge topics include:

- Climate and weather
- Climate zones
- Seasons
- How the Earth's atmosphere keeps us warm
- Ecosystems 'dance' in time with the rhythm of the seasons
- Ecosystems and climate change

Part 1: Subject knowledge

Difference between climate and weather

The difference between weather and climate can be confusing. When we think about the weather, we automatically think of specific events, such as a rainy day or strong winds, that we can picture in our minds. When describing the climate, we are not describing a particular event; we are describing trends or patterns in the behaviour of the weather over a period of time. For example, where I live in the UK, I would describe the climate as generally mild but often wet and windy. Summers tend to be warm, and winters are normally

DOI: 10.4324/9781003166276-4

cool, rather than cold. When describing the climate, we are describing the average or established behaviour of the weather over many years. Of course, sometimes the weather bucks the trend, and we may experience a heatwave in summer or heavy snow in winter. However, it is very unlikely these conditions will prevail for more than a few weeks.

UK climate

Generally, Britain experiences cool, wet winters and warm, wet summers and only rarely experiences extremes of heat or cold, drought or wind. The weather conditions in the UK are also very changeable. For example, I am writing this in October and for the next three days the BBC forecasts a sunny day today, heavy clouds and light rain tomorrow, and thundery showers the day after.

Although the climate is generally similar across the UK, there are differences in weather patterns in different regions. For example, the Southeast has cold winters and warm and dry summers, compared to the very wet winters and warm and wet summers in the Southwest. The Northwest has mild winters, cool summers, and heavy rain all year, while the Northeast has cold winters, cool summers, and steady rain throughout the year.

Climate zones

The climate varies in different parts of the world. Generally, the further away from the equator we go, the colder the climate. This is because the Sun shines more directly on equatorial regions than on other parts of the world. The polar regions experience the coldest temperatures on the planet. The northern polar region is mostly frozen ocean surrounded by land masses. Temperatures range from 0°C to 20°C in summer, while winters are icy cold with temperatures below -60°C. The southern polar region is a vast continent of mountains and high plateaus buried under more than 3 km of ice. Its climate is colder than the north, with temperatures often dipping to below -80°C. The interior of the region is a dry, frozen desert, with plant life mainly found in the coastal regions. The interior hardly has any surviving animal life.

As we move away from the polar regions towards the equator, climates generally get warmer. Equatorial climates are home to the world's rainforests, where rainfall and humidity are high. Temperatures vary between 25–35°C, with the hottest months varying little from the cooler months by only two to three degrees. Being close to the equator, the length of day and night hardly varies throughout the year. People who live in equatorial climates tend to describe their weather in terms of wet and dry seasons, rather than the four seasons experienced in other parts of the world.

Equatorial rainforests create their own climate

Plants have evolved to suit the climate where they live. For example, plants in arid regions store moisture in their fleshy leaves or have developed extensive root systems to make the most of the limited rainfall. On the other hand, plants that grow in warm, wet equatorial rainforests develop thick leaves with drip tips and wax surfaces to allow the copious rainfall to run off onto the ground to prevent rotting. Most of the available nutrients in a rainforest are in the top layer of the soil, so the roots of the trees are often

Figure 4.1 Rainforest tree with buttress roots

relatively close to the surface. Wide buttress roots help support the trees and also take up nutrients.

Having adapted to the climate, plants also have the potential to affect the climate due to the release of water vapour during photosynthesis. For example, rainforests release huge amounts of water vapour into the air, which can lead to the formation of clouds. These clouds have the potential to reduce the amount of sunlight that can reach the Earth's surface and increase rainfall. Rainforests can have a major influence on the climate. Forests in equatorial and temperate regions have a cooling effect, while boreal forests in higher northern latitudes make their climate warmer.

The Eden Project website provides the following summary of how rainforests help regulate the Earth's climate:

- Air movers: Rainforests enhance the rise of warm, moist air. This powers winds which circulate air around the world.
- Sun reflectors: Massive white clouds form above rainforests which reflect sunlight.
- Rain makers: Rainforests make rain and rain makes rainforests.
- Water sweaters: Water evaporates (transpires) from leaves. This has a cooling effect (just like sweating).
- Carbon catchers: Forests take in carbon dioxide from the air as they grow.
- Flood defenders: Rainforest roots and soil hold onto water like a sponge.

Temperate climates

The UK experiences a temperate climate. Temperate climates occur in the middle latitudes between the tropics and the polar regions. Places in temperate zones are characterised by relatively moderate average temperatures, with temperatures averaging

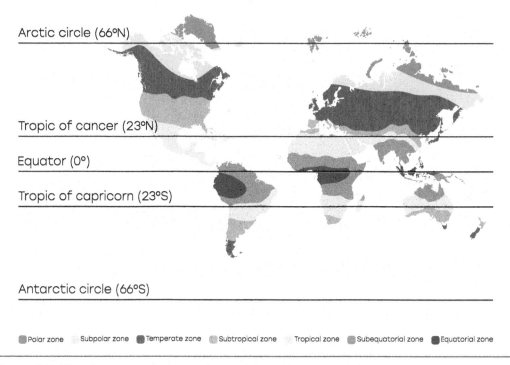

Arctic circle (66°N)

Tropic of cancer (23°N)

Equator (0°)

Tropic of capricorn (23°S)

Antarctic circle (66°S)

Polar zone   Subpolar zone   Temperate zone   Subtropical zone   Tropical zone   Subequatorial zone   Equatorial zone

Figure 4.2 Climate zones

above 10°C in summer and above -3°C in winter. Temperate regions are the most popular to live in, as they do not experience the extremes of temperature of some other climates. The ability to grow a large variety of crops is a major advantage for people living in these regions. Natural vegetation includes both deciduous and coniferous forests.

Seasons

People living in temperate climates experience four distinct seasons. These seasonal changes in weather are due to the tilt of the Earth's axis relative to the Sun, causing the intensity of sunlight received by the northern and southern hemispheres to change throughout the year.

As the Earth moves around the Sun, the part of the Earth tilting towards the Sun receives the most sunlight. When the northern hemisphere is angled towards the Sun, rays of sunlight shine directly onto this part of the Earth, creating longer days and warmer summer weather. In contrast, southern regions experience less daylight and colder winter weather because they are tilted away from the Sun. As the Earth continues around the Sun, the situation changes until the northern hemisphere is tilted away from the Sun, creating winter conditions. Consequently, regions in the southern hemisphere experience summer temperatures as they are angled towards the Sun. Because the direction of the Earth's tilt always remains the same, the southern hemisphere experiences opposite seasons to the north.

EARTH'S SEASONS

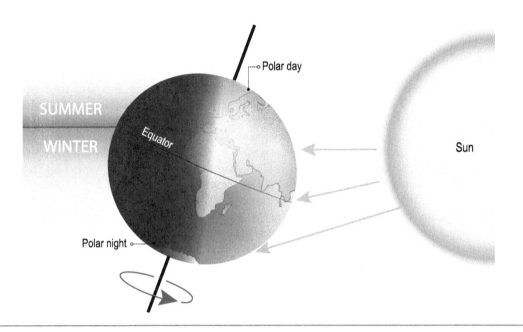

Figure 4.3 Tilt of the Earth's axis

The differences in the seasons are most distinct in the polar regions, where they only experience sunlight for six months of the year. On the other hand, the tilt of the Earth does not significantly affect the intensity of light that falls on areas around the equator, where people identify different seasons by the amount of rain they receive.

Astronomical and meteorological seasons

Dividing the year into seasons helps us make sense of and prepare for the changing weather. Knowing the seasons is especially useful for farmers and gardeners for planting crops. The word 'season' comes from the Latin word 'sationem', meaning 'sowing'.

The dates for the start of the seasons depend on whether you are referring to the astronomical or meteorological system. Astronomical seasons refer to the position of Earth's orbit in relation to the Sun, as discussed earlier. For example, astronomical spring begins on or around the 20th of March and ends on or around the 21st of June. Due to the elliptical orbit of the Earth around the Sun, the seasons are not all the same length.

Meteorological seasons are not just based on the orbit of the Earth, but also take into account how average temperatures change throughout the year. The meteoro-logical system divides the year into three-month periods, with each season starting at the beginning of the first month. For example, on the meteorological calendar, spring will always start on 1 March and end on 31 May. The seasons are defined as spring (March, April, May), summer (June, July, August), autumn (September, October, November) and winter (December, January, February). Summer and winter are predicted to be the hottest and coldest months, while the autumn and spring months are times of change.

How the Earth's atmosphere keeps us warm

Throughout the seasons, the Sun provides the energy we need to live and to warm up our planet. However, the Earth would be a lot colder if it wasn't for the greenhouse gases in the atmosphere that trap the Sun's heat and prevent it escaping back into space. The atmosphere is made up of a mixture of gases, mainly nitrogen and oxygen, with a small amount of carbon dioxide and other gases. Carbon dioxide is called a greenhouse gas because it acts like a greenhouse. It lets the Sun's heat through to warm up the sea and land, but prevents it escaping again back into space.

A greenhouse keeps warm by trapping heat from the Sun. When the Sun's rays pass through the glass, the heat is absorbed by the air, floor, and all the other things inside. Much of this heat is then trapped because it cannot escape back through the glass. Therefore, the temperature inside a greenhouse is warmer than the outside. The same goes for the Earth: the temperature inside the Earth's atmosphere is warmer than that outside in space. The atmosphere is like a big blanket wrapped around the Earth, keeping it warm and controlling the climate and the weather.

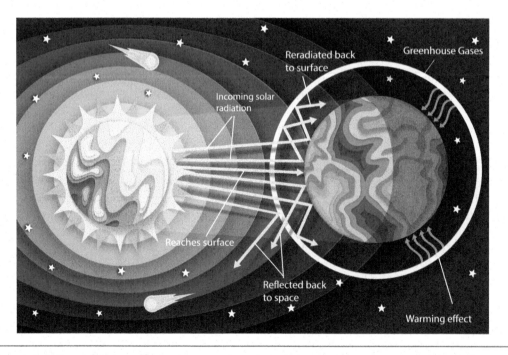

Figure 4.4 Greenhouse effect

Ecosystems 'dance' in time with the rhythm of the seasons

Throughout the year, nature's rhythms guide our own behaviour and the behaviour of the natural world. Nature's rhythms include the rising and setting of the Sun and Moon, the changing light and temperatures from day to night, and the weather patterns from season to season.

Temperate woodlands provide good examples of how the behaviour of wildlife is orchestrated by the rhythm of the changing seasons. Spring is the time when the woodland wakes up from its winter's rest. With renewed vitality wildflowers burst out, taking advantage of the spring sunshine before the leaves on the trees grow big enough to steal the Sun's energy. In summer, trees monopolise the sunlight to grow and produce their fruit. In autumn, the woodland prepares for the coming winter. Fruits ripen and seeds are distributed in the hope of creating offspring to maintain the species into the future. As the days grow colder and winter approaches, deciduous trees shed their leaves and take a rest in preparation for the year to come. Winter is the time for the woodland to tidy itself up. Leaves and dead wood that litter the ground are broken down by invertebrates such as woodlice, snails, and worms, and decomposed by fungi and bacteria. Nothing is wasted. Having returned to the soil, the decomposed leaf litter provides nutrients for plants to grow when spring comes around, and life in the woodland continues its 'dance' in time to the rhythm of the seasons.

Figure 4.5 Spring in a woodland
Source: Anna Loxley

Ecosystems and climate change

When we talk about an ecosystem, we are describing a complex web of interdependent animals and plants living together in particular environmental conditions. The climate has a major influence on the wellbeing of wildlife within an ecosystem. Changes to the climate can have serious effects, such as drought, flooding, and wildfires, and may disturb the timing and rhythm of the seasons.

Woodland ecosystems are delicately balanced, and events are orchestrated by the steady rhythm of the changing seasons. If this rhythm is disrupted by changes in the climate, then events within the ecosystem may no longer be synchronised. Take for example the woodland ecosystem. Spring is the signal for bluebells and other wildflowers to grow. Their flowers provide early food for bees and butterflies. Timing is everything. If, because of climate change, the pollinators emerge before the wildflowers are in bloom, then they may struggle to survive. This could lead to a reduction in the number of pollinators available to pollinate trees and shrubs, whose seeds and fruit are eaten by birds and small mammals. Consequently, fewer pollinators mean less food for primary consumers, which in turn affects secondary consumers higher up the food chain. Climate change is already affecting the rhythm of the seasons. Spring weather is arriving earlier and lasting longer. As a result, the behaviour of wildlife is becoming less predictable, and in some cases species' lives are no longer synchronised with those they rely on in their ecosystem.

Part 2: Working toward the big idea

In this part, models of good practice enable children to work on their understanding of the processes that shape the Earth's climate. Children's learning starts by establishing the difference between climate and weather, and by comparing the climate in different parts of the world. The greenhouse effect is introduced to explain how the Earth traps heat energy from the Sun to warm its surface and control the climate. Children also explore how the orientation of Earth, as it orbits the Sun, creates the temperatures associated with the different seasons. These ideas feed into their understanding of how climate change can irreparably damage delicately balanced ecosystems by disturbing the rhythm of the seasons.

Children have opportunities to develop and use the following science and design technology skills:

- Work collaboratively towards common goals.
- Use different types of scientific enquiries, including data gathering and fair testing.
- Research using secondary sources.
- Generate, develop, model, and communicate ideas through discussion, sketches, and prototypes.
- Communicate outcomes of their research, enquiry, and design in different ways.
- Apply their learning in real-life contexts.

Health and safety

Follow the health and safety guidelines in the ASE publication *Be Safe!* when:

- planning a visit to the woodlands (Studies out of the classroom p12)
- using mains electricity (Using electrical equipment p28).

Exploring children's ideas

Talk! Weather memories

In small groups, children share their weather memories of a holiday which was adversely affected by the weather. Their stories should start with where they went, what type of weather they expected, how things went wrong, and what they did to make the best of the holiday. Bring the class together and talk about how they normally chose their holiday destinations. How do they know in advance what the weather will be like? Which places are normally sunny? Do they think Iceland is good place for a beach holiday? Talk together about places where the weather is normally warm and sunny, and compare them with places where it is normally cold and wet. Introduce the term 'climate' to mean normal weather. For example, the climate in Spain in summer is hot and dry. How would they describe the climate in the UK in summer?

Figure 4.6 Sydney Harbour, Australia

Planning a holiday to Australia

Working in groups, children plan a month-long holiday to Australia to include visits to Melbourne, Sydney, Darwin, and Perth. The planning should include choosing the best time of the year for the trip and the types of clothes they need to take. Because of baggage restrictions, they are only allowed to take one small bag for their clothes. Groups create posters which depict the main attractions of each city, their climates, and the clothing they intend to take. Groups present and compare their posters. Encourage children to justify the types of clothes they have chosen with respect to the climatic conditions expected in each city. On what information have they based their decisions?

Talk! Climate

Talk about climate as a description of average weather conditions, and how the climate describes trends or patterns in the behaviour of the weather over a period of time. For example, the UK climate is generally wet, with cool winters and warm summers.

Ask the children to describe the climate where they live. Bring all the ideas together and agree on a description of the local climate. Create space for a local climate display. Start with the children's description of the local climate, and each week add a weather photograph taken in the local area. Annotate the photographs with weather stories for that week. Continue taking photographs for the display throughout the year, and identify trends in the weather for each term. Talk about whether their experience of the local climate is different from the official version for their region provided by the Met Office. At the end of each term, reassess the classes' description of the local climate.

The ideal climate

Ask children to describe their ideal climate. Do they prefer hot weather, warm weather, or cold weather? Would they prefer less rain and more sunshine? Are they fed up with the way the weather is always changing in the UK? Perhaps they would like to live in a part of the world where the weather is nearly always the same? Children form groups with similar preferences, and use the web to discover places in the world with their 'ideal' climates. Groups take on the role of international estate agents, and produce illustrated pamphlets designed to help them sell their ideal destination to people who want to move abroad. Groups come together to present and justify their ideas.

Research! Climate zones

Working in small groups, children use information sources to compare the climates of different parts of the world. Children divide the world into zones with similar climates. Groups come together to present their ideas and create a display of the Earth's climate zones.

Figure 4.7 The ideal climate? San Diego, California

Talking points: true, false, or not sure?

- All the hottest places are in the southern hemisphere.
- The Arctic is the wettest place on Earth.
- The Arctic and Antarctic are deserts.
- Places near the equator have summer all year long.
- Deserts are the hottest places on Earth.
- Tropical rainforests are the wettest places on Earth.
- It rains more over the oceans than on land.

Groups discuss and try to reach agreement on their responses to the talking points. Use their ideas as starting points for further discussion about the world's climate. Contact schools in different climate zones to exchange climate data. Establish links with other primary schools around the world to share the work you are doing on climate change.

Information sources

Websites

- Arctic region (arcticcentre.org)
- Climate zones – Met Office

- Educate (esa.int) (climate)
- Investigating climate zones and climate change (geography.org.uk)
- Our resources for 7–11-year-olds – Met Office
- Rainforest Ecosystem – Types, Characteristics, Benefits. – ImportantIndia.com

Working on scientific understanding

Children work on their understanding of how the tilt of the Earth creates the seasons as it orbits the Sun. They also learn about how greenhouse gases in the atmosphere control the Earth's climate.

Talk! Seasons

Start this part by talking about the seasons. Ask children to compare the weather in autumn, winter, spring, and summer. Encourage them to speculate about why the weather is generally colder in winter than in summer.

Talking points: true, false, or not sure?

- It is colder in winter because the Sun is further away from the Earth than in summer.
- It is warmer in summer because the Sun shines brighter than in winter.
- It is warmer in summer than winter because the Earth rotates on its axis.
- It is warmer in summer than winter because the Earth moves around the Sun.
- It is colder in winter because the Moon blocks out the Sun.
- It is cold in winter and warm in summer because of the tilt of the Earth.
- When it is winter in the UK, it is summer in Australia.

Groups discuss the talking points and try to agree on how to respond. Encourage them to provide reasons for their ideas. Use their responses to assess what they know about how the seasons are created. Address major misconceptions.

Talk about how the differences in temperature from season to season are caused by the tilt of the Earth. Owing to the tilt of the Earth's axis, the intensity of sunlight received by the northern and southern hemispheres changes throughout the year as the Earth orbits the Sun. Use video clips from the web to illustrate how the seasons are created.

Model! Seasonal weather

Children start by modelling day and night. Provide groups with a globe (Earth) and a torch (Sun). In a darkened room, ask them to model how the spin of the Earth creates day and night. In this model, the Sun remains stationary and the Earth spins on its axis. At any one time, part of the Earth is lit up by light from the Sun, and the other part will

Figure 4.8 Sunrise over the Earth

be in shadow. Identify areas of the world where it is night when it is day in the UK. Also, model times of the day such as dawn, midday, and twilight, and further illustrate by showing children pictures of the Sun in the sky at these times.

Now challenge the groups to model winter and summer in the UK. Start by showing them an image of the Earth's tilt, and explain that the tilt remains in the same direction as the Earth moves around the Sun. Allow time for groups to work out ways of modelling the seasons using a globe and a torch. Groups come together to share their ideas. Talk together and reinforce how seasons are caused by the tilt of the Earth's axis as it moves around the Sun. Show them that when the North Pole tilts towards the Sun it receives sunlight for 24 hours each day, and when in winter it is pointing away from the Sun it hardly gets any sunlight at all as it spins on its axis. Also, demonstrate how the tilt of the Earth makes little difference in the amount of light that shines on the equator throughout the year. Talk about why equatorial regions do not experience distinct seasons. Use video clip animations to further develop children's understanding.

Changing seasons

Add to children's understanding of seasons by talking about autumn and spring as times of change from summer to winter, and winter back to summer. Discuss the following timeline:

- Summer solstice: The start of summer and the longest day of the year
- Autumn equinox: The start of autumn, when day and night have equal length
- Winter solstice: The start of winter and the shortest day of the year
- Spring equinox: The start of spring, when day and night have equal length

Model the summer solstice, autumn equinox, winter solstice, and the spring equinox. Talk about how they naturally mark the start of the seasons. These astronomical dates for the start of each season are different to the ones used by meteorologists. Children can compare the dates for the astronomical seasons with those chosen by the meteorologists. Can children discover why the meteorologists choose different dates?

Thought experiment

Ask children to imagine what the climate would be like in the UK if the Earth's axis was not tilted. In other words, what would happen if it was always at the same perpendicular angle to its direction of motion around the Sun? Children create their own models to explain their ideas.

Puzzle! Do other planets have seasons?

Provide children with the task of discovering whether other planets have seasons. Talk about the link between the tilt of the Earth and the seasons. Does this mean that planets which have a tilt will also have seasons? All the planets in our solar system have tilts: does this mean they all have seasons? Listen to children's ideas. Groups can compare the tilts and the climates of different planets, and try to discover whether they all have seasons. Can they find a relationship between the size of the tilt and how temperatures change from season to season? Are the lengths of the seasons connected to the time the planet takes to orbit the Sun?

Figure 4.9 NASA's Perseverance Rover
Source: NASA Image and Video Library

Groups compare the atmosphere and climate on Earth with those on Mars. Mars has a tilt of 25.19 degrees compared to the Earth's 23.44 degrees. This small difference has a huge effect on the difference between summer and winter temperatures. In winter, temperatures near the poles can fall to -125°C, while in summer temperatures at the equator may rise to 20°C during the day, although they can plummet at night. On Earth, the difference between corresponding temperatures is not so large.

Mars is a wonderful place for children to explore. In recent years, NASA has landed a number of rovers on the Martian surface, each sending back amazing photographs. NASA has recently sent their latest robotic explorer, named Perseverance, which is searching for evidence of life on Mars. Children can join in the quest to find life on Mars by visiting NASA's Perseverance website. They can also check out the seasonal weather on the Curiosity website.

Mission to Mars

Children plan their own mission to Mars. Talk about what they would like to find out. For example, NASA has discovered a liquid water lake underneath the southern polar ice cap. Is it possible life could exist in this lake? Scientists here on Earth have found life in lakes deep under the ice sheets in Antarctica. Therefore, it could be possible that life exists, or did exist, in the lake found on Mars.

Children can plan an ambitious expedition to land a robotic explorer on Mars' southern ice cap to look for signs of life. Even NASA hasn't done this yet! They could design an explorer to drill down and take samples of ice at different levels. The mission should carry out observations of the weather, including seasonal temperatures, wind speeds and hours of sunlight. They could also search for water under the ice, but this is likely to be a long way down. Groups design all aspects of their robotic explorers including the landing gear, the types of instruments it needs, and how it will travel over the ice.

Figure 4.10 Sunrise on Mars

Before they start designing their Mars explorer, groups should use NASA websites to study the robotic explorers that have already been sent to Mars. Also encourage them to use the web to discover places on Earth where life has been found in lakes beneath the ice sheets. Based on what they find, children can get some idea of the types of organisms that might live under the ice on Mars. Groups report on the 'findings' of their mission in the style of a popular science newspaper article. Encourage children to be imaginative within the realms of what might be possible.

Talk! Living in a greenhouse

Start by asking children if any of them have a greenhouse at home. What do they use it for? What can they say about the temperature inside a greenhouse compared to

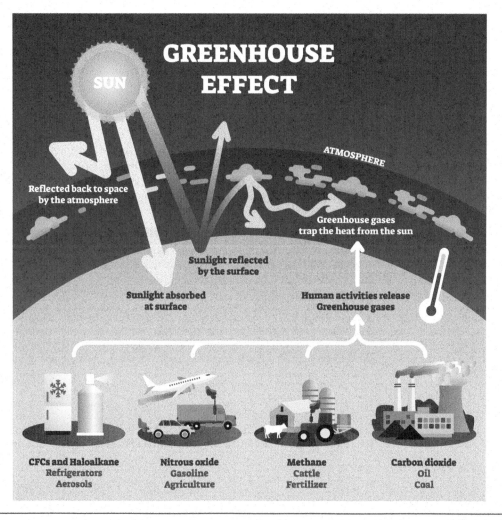

Figure 4.11 Greenhouse effect

the outside? Listen to children's experiences. Talk together about how a greenhouse works. Focus on the idea that it traps heat, so it is always warmer inside than outside. In groups, children discuss the advantages and disadvantages of living in a giant greenhouse. Bring the groups together and talk about their ideas. Talk together about how we would be warmer in the greenhouse in winter, but it might be too hot in the summer.

Compare living on Earth to living in a greenhouse. Use images to show how the Earth is surrounded by a 'blanket' of air which acts like the glass in a greenhouse. Gases in the air enable energy from the Sun to pass through them and warm up the Earth's surface, but at the same time prevent heat emitted from the Earth escaping back into space. These gases are called greenhouse gases, and without them the Earth would be a much colder place. Remind children that the atmosphere is made up of a mixture of gases, mainly nitrogen and oxygen, with a small amount of carbon dioxide and other gases. Explain that carbon dioxide is the main greenhouse gas because of the warming effect it has on the Earth. Ask children to predict what might happen if more and more carbon dioxide is added to the air. Make the point that the more carbon dioxide there is in the atmosphere, the warmer the planet is likely to be. Illustrate the greenhouse effect using animations and images from the web. More information is in Part 1.

Model! Greenhouse effect

Working in groups, children use a glass jar to make a model greenhouse. With the glass jar laying on its side, they add some sand to represent the Earth. Then, pierce a hole in the lid, just big enough to insert a thermometer, and seal the jar. Using a small lamp to represent the Sun, children can warm up the Earth and air inside the jar. Use another thermometer to measure the air temperature outside the greenhouse. Groups take temperature readings as the 'Earth' warms up and plot the results on a graph. Compare increases in temperatures inside and outside the jar. Turn the lamp off and continue to take temperature readings. How long does the temperature inside the greenhouse remain above the outside air temperature? Talk about how the greenhouse traps the heat energy.

Enquire! Earth's atmosphere

Children investigate how carbon dioxide warms up the planet by modelling the Earth's atmosphere. This can be done using a sealable glass jar, bicarbonate of soda, vinegar, and a thermometer to measure the temperature inside the jar. Carbon dioxide is produced when the bicarbonate of soda and vinegar are mixed together in the bottom of the jar, simulating the increase of greenhouse gas in the atmosphere. Children use a small lamp to represent the Sun to warm up the 'atmosphere'. Allow them to plan their own experiments to investigate the effect increased levels of carbon dioxide have on the temperature of the 'atmosphere' inside the jar. Talk about the need for a control experiment, i.e: a jar with just air. Encourage them to continue recording data after the 'Sun' is switched off.

Groups come together to present and share their results. Talk about the effects carbon dioxide has on the atmosphere inside the jar. Children should find that the air in the jar reaches a higher temperature when mixed with carbon dioxide than when it is filled with air alone. It also cools down more slowly when the light source is turned off. Compare the model to the real world. Heating the model represents daytime, and turning the light off represents night. Talk about how increasing the amount of carbon dioxide in the air can alter the daily heating and cooling of the Earth. Children learn more about global warming in Chapter 6.

Information sources

Websites

- Discovery of an underground lake on Mars stokes hopes of finding life – Bing video
- Do other planets have seasons? – BBC Bitesize
- Earth Minute Videos | Explore – Climate Change: Vital Signs of the Planet (nasa.gov)
- Mars 2020 Perseverance Rover – NASA Mars
- Mars Express Views Red Planet's South Pole – NASA's Mars Exploration Program
- Mars 2003 | NASA Image and Video Library
- NASA's Perseverance rover has just landed on Mars (nationalgeographic.com)
- New Lifeforms Found Deep Beneath Antarctica Are "Breaking All the Rules" | IFLScience
- Perseverance on Mars | NASA Image and Video Library
- Seasons – Met Office
- Video: Why Do We Have Different Seasons? | Habitat Earth (calacademy.org)

Books

- Loxley, P., Dawes, L., Nicholls, L., Dore, B. (2018) *Teaching Primary Science*. Abingdon: Routledge.
- Loxley, P. (2018) *Practical Ideas for Teaching Primary Science*. Abingdon: Routledge.

The bigger picture

Children explore how living things within an ecosystem depend on climate, and in particular how they are adapted to the rhythm of the seasons.

Talk! Nature's rhythms

Start by talking about how nature's rhythms guide our own behaviour and the behaviour of the natural world. First, focus on the rising and setting of the Sun. What impact do those daily rhythms have on children's behaviour? What would life be like if the

Sun shone all the time? Listen to children's ideas, and explore how they think the daily rhythms of night and day affect the natural world.

Working in groups, children use information sources to discover which woodland animals are active at night and which are active during the day. Are there any animals that are active both day and night? (Other than humans, that is!) Groups present their findings to the rest of the class, and talk about the advantages and disadvantages of the lifestyles of different animals.

Talk! Rhythms of the seasons

Focus children's attention on the rhythms of the seasons. Ask children to list all the ways that their behaviour throughout the year is in tune with the different seasons. What do they do in summer, which they do not do in winter? In which season are they most active? Do the different seasons affect their moods? Which is their favourite season? How do they think the different seasons influence the behaviour of animals and plants? Talk about whether wildlife is in tune with the rhythms of the seasons.

Enquire! How do woodlands respond to the rhythm of the seasons?

Arrange visits to the local woodland throughout the seasons, so children can record how the wildlife responds to changes in temperature and hours of sunlight. In spring, the woodland responds to the warmer days and increased sunlight after winter, and in autumn, it responds to the onset of cooler weather and shorter days.

Take magnifiers, sweep nets, pooters, and binoculars. Children record their findings by taking photographs, using voice recorders, taking notes, and making sketches. Impress on the children they should work scientifically. This means they observe and

Figure 4.12 Seasons

record things carefully, ask questions, and make sure they do not damage the woodland. Avoid using tick lists. Provide time for children to explore and discover answers to their questions. Talk together about whether the animals they observe are primary, secondary, or tertiary consumers. Sketch out simple food webs.

After each visit, children present their findings and describe how the woodland is responding to the seasonal temperatures. What influence have they had on plant growth and animal activity compared to the last visit? Presentations should include food webs which exemplify feeding relationships in the woodland.

At an appropriate time, groups compare their observations from their woodland visits, and prepare displays to show how the woodland ecosystem is orchestrated by the rhythm of the seasons. Use children's observations to help them picture the role climate plays in synchronising the behaviour of the living things in the woodland ecosystem. Talk about how bees emerge from hibernation at the same time the wildflowers bloom in spring, ensuring a plentiful supply of pollen and nectar. The behaviour of blue tits is another example of how nature dances to the beat of the seasons. Most blue tits build their nest in late March, about the time buds on the trees start bursting into leaf. This coincides with the time tiny caterpillars hatch to feast on the fresh tree leaves. Blue tits depend on the caterpillars to feed their chicks, each of which can demand up to 100 caterpillars a day. Ask children to speculate what might happen to the blue tits and bees if the climate changed and the rhythm of the seasons could no longer be predicted. What will happen if the bees emerge before the wildflowers are in bloom, and caterpillars hatch before the trees burst into leaf? Children use information sources to discover how other types of woodland animals might be affected by climate change. Children explore more about climate change in the next chapter.

Paint! Rhythms of the seasons

Children paint a series of pictures depicting the woodland at different time of the year. If possible, they should paint the same view of the woodland each time, paying close attention to the changes created by the rhythm of seasons. Encourage children to be creative and use their imaginations to capture not only changes to the physical landscape, but also changes to the weather and the atmosphere in the woodland. Create a major display of the children's work and invite the local community to view it. Publish children's work on the school's preferred social media platform.

Enquire! Nature's Calendar

Children can help scientists track the effects of climate change on the behaviour of birds and pollinators by taking part in the Woodland Trust Nature's Calendar project.

> Our climate is changing. Climate change will produce some winners which are well adapted to climate change and some losers which cannot adapt quickly enough. Long-term monitoring of species like blackbird will help scientists to gain a greater understanding of this issue, and provide policymakers with hard evidence.
>
> (Woodland Trust Website)

The project involves looking out for signs that the rhythm of the seasons is changing. For example, children log when certain leaf buds burst, when they see the season's first butterfly, when certain birds start to build their nests, when certain trees start to drop their leaves and when fruit starts to ripen on particular plants. By collecting and submitting the data, children will be contributing to a long biological record that dates back as far as 1736. Information about the project can be found on the Woodland Trust website, with details of all the different animals and plants children can record.

Information sources

Websites

- BBC – Earth – In spring the UK is a migration hotspot
- Do All Birds Migrate? | Different Types of Migratory Birds – The RSPB
- Nature's Calendar – Woodland Trust
- Shaping our Future | WWF
- Spring – Met Office
- UK Native Trees – Woodland Trust
- When Do Bluebells Flower? – Woodland Trust
- When Do Blue Tits Nest? – Woodland Trust
- Where Do Bees Go in Winter? – Woodland Trust
- Which birds migrate? Who to spot this summer – Woodland Trust

Books

- Loxley, P., Dawes, L., Nicholls, L., and Dore, B. (2018) *Teaching Primary Science*. Abingdon: Routledge.
- Loxley, P. (2018) *Practical Ideas for Teaching Primary Science*. Abingdon: Routledge.

CHAPTER 5

CLIMATE CHANGE

Big idea: *Climate change is a long-term shift in average weather patterns across the world, caused by human activity.*

This chapter builds on ideas about weather and climate to develop children's understanding of the science of climate change. Part 1 provides subject knowledge for teachers concerning the evidence for climate change and its causes. Part 2 sets out models of good practice which provide ideas and activities teachers can use to organise children's learning of the big idea. The ideas presented provide a real-life context to extend and enrich the primary curriculum.

The topics include:

- Climate change
- Evidence for climate change
- Causes of climate change
- The science of burning
- Methane is a greenhouse gas
- How digestion causes methane
- Carbon footprints

Part 1: Subject knowledge

Climate change

Climate change is the long-term shift in average weather patterns across the world. Since the start of the Industrial Revolution in the middle of the 18th century, we have been polluting the air with particles and gases which have caused global temperatures to rise, resulting in long-term changes to the climate.

DOI: 10.4324/9781003166276-5

Birmingham.

Figure 5.1 Historic view of Birmingham (Wood engraving, 1893)

Before the Industrial Revolution, people produced goods on a very small scale in their homes; this produced little air pollution. At this time, the average temperature across the world was stable at around 14°C, as it had been for the previous 11,000 years. The Industrial Revolution started the burning of large amounts of fossil fuels such as coal, oil, and gas, which continues today. Burning fossil fuels produces the large amounts of energy needed for the mass production of goods, but also releases huge amounts of polluting chemicals and gases into the air. These gases continue to build up in the atmosphere and are contributing to the processes which shape our weather and climate. For example, in recent times the level of carbon dioxide in the atmosphere has risen by 40%, which is higher than it has been for the last 800,000 years. Evidence collected by scientists has shown that these high levels of industrial gases in the atmosphere are the main cause of the increases in global temperatures.

Evidence for climate change

The evidence for rapid climate change is compelling. Global temperatures are rising, oceans are warming, sea levels are rising, ice sheets are shrinking, and glaciers are retreating almost everywhere in the world. Scientists have observed that global heatwaves and major weather events, such as hurricanes, are happening more often and becoming more intensive. Cold spells are decreasing, but heavy rain in some regions of the world is more frequent and more extreme. There is also an increase in global drought, with the prospect of worsening drought in many parts of the world in the decades ahead.

Records show that over the last 60 years, the rate of global warming has been steadily increasing. Scientists have reported that 17 of the 18 warmest years ever recorded have occurred in the 21st century, with each of the last 3 decades being warmer than the previous one. Based on their climate change models, scientists predict that the world could become 4.8°C warmer by the end of this century if we don't drastically reduce greenhouse gas emissions.

Modelling is an important tool for climate scientists. Climate models are mock-ups that simulate the behaviour of the weather over a chosen period of time. Scientists feed data collected from Earth-orbiting satellites and ground-based sources into super-computer models, which enable them to predict how the world's climates are likely to change in the future. The models tell us that the climate is changing, and there is a greater than 95% probability that the causes are due to human activity.

Climatologists use their models to simulate the effects on the climate of releasing large amounts of greenhouse gases in the air. At the same time, they can also simulate what the climate would be like if the air were not clogged up with those gases. If they compare their simulations with what actually happened to the climate over a set period of time, they can draw conclusions about the causes of global warming. Based on experience, extensive data, and powerful modelling, most scientists are convinced that human activity is irreversibly changing the climate.

Our planet is warming at an alarming rate

Since the Industrial Revolution, the average temperature at the Earth's surface has risen by around 1°C. This is a rapid change, as our global climate naturally changes much more slowly. In different parts of the world the rise is considerably higher.

The highest increases are in the Arctic, where the average temperature has gone up by 2.3°C since the 1970s. In recent years, the Arctic region has experienced its highest temperatures ever recorded. In June 2020, the small Siberian town of Verkhoyansk was reported to have experienced a scorching daytime high of 38°C, a record for inside the Arctic Circle. This is 18°C higher than the average maximum daily temperature in June. A team of scientists from Oxford University found that June 2020 in Siberia was 5°C warmer than any June from 1981 to 2010. Their study shows that man-made climate change was mostly likely the cause of it. In fact, they worked out that greenhouse gases were 600 times more likely than natural causes to have made this Siberian heatwave.

Heat waves across the world

More intense and frequent heat waves around the world provide further evidence of climate change. In 2021, record high temperatures were recorded in Siberia, Western United States, Canada, Northern and Eastern Europe, Northeast China, and Japan. July 2021 was the hottest July since records began 142 years ago.

Canada weather: Heat hits record 46.6C as US north-west also sizzles

> Canada has recorded its highest ever temperature as the country's west and the US Pacific north-west frazzle in an unprecedented heatwave. Lytton in British Columbia soared to 46.6C (116F) on Sunday, breaking an 84-year-old record, officials said. The US and Canada have both warned citizens of "dangerous" heat levels that could persist this week. Experts say that

climate change is expected to increase the frequency of extreme weather events, such as heatwaves.

BBC News online, June 2021

Extreme heat cooked mussels, clams, and other shellfish live on beaches in Western Canada, where temperatures soared to a record high of close to 50°C in late June 2021. At least 134 people died in the Vancouver area due to the dangerous heat levels. The extreme heat, combined with intense drought, caused large-scale fires to break out in woodland areas, and in towns, officials were forced to set up temporary water fountains and misting stations on street corners. At the same time it hit Canada, the heat wave also hit Greece, Siberia, and other places across the world. Land temperatures in the Arctic Circle soared to 48°C, in what scientists are calling a 'persistent heat' wave in Siberia.

How is the climate changing in the UK?

Average temperatures in the UK have risen by about 0.8°C in the last 60 years. Some of the warmest years in the UK have occurred since 1990, with the 10 hottest years since 1884 happening in the last 17 years. The climate does not get warmer every year, but there is a clear trend of increasing temperatures around the country. Summers are getting hotter and drier with more frequent heatwaves, while on average winters are getting warmer but wetter. Natural variations causing unusually cold years still happen,

Figure 5.2 Canadian town of Lytton burnt to the ground by wildfires

but these events are becoming less likely. Heavy rainfall is also becoming more common. Since 1998, the UK has experienced the ten wettest years on record. All the changes in the UK's weather patterns are thought by scientists to be linked to global climate change, and are likely to accelerate in the future.

Causes of climate change

Plants absorb the Sun's energy and use it to produce the organic, carbon-based material from which they are made. The Sun's energy is then passed on to animals when they eat the plants. When plants and animals die and are buried in the ground, energy stored in their organic material is buried with them. This is the way fossil fuels store energy from the Sun, which is released when they are burnt.

Technologies such as power stations, motor cars, and aeroplanes, which burn fossil fuels, release carbon dioxide into the air. The carbon dioxide, together with other greenhouse gases, forms a 'gas blanket' around the Earth which prevents heat from the ground escaping into space. At the same time, the Sun's rays are able to pass through the layers of carbon dioxide to heat the ground. This heat is then trapped by the blanket of carbon dioxide. Carbon dioxide is a major greenhouse gas which causes global warming. Refer to Chapter 4 for a description of the greenhouse effect.

Burning fossil fuels also releases sulphur dioxide and nitrogen oxides into the air. When combined with rainwater, these gases contribute to the formation of acid rain, making the rainwater corrosive. Acid rain can have adverse effects on lakes, streams, and wetlands, killing insects and aquatic animals such as fish, crayfish, and clams. The demise of insects

Figure 5.3 Coal-fired power station

Figure 5.4 Trees killed by acid rain

and aquatic animals within the ecosystems affects birds, amphibians, and mammals that feed on them. Acid rain also damages soils and forests. The acid destroys essential nutrients in the soil, making it more difficult for plants to grow. It can also damage the leaves of trees and other plants, leaving them more vulnerable to disease, insects, and cold weather. Acid rain can also affect a plant's ability to reproduce. It can damage buildings, bridges, and other infrastructure by corroding paint work and weathering stone structures. It can also damage people's health, especially those with breathing problems such as asthma.

The science of burning

One of the earliest scientific attempts to explain burning was made by Johannes Baptista van Helmont (1580–1644), a Flemish physician and alchemist. Van Helmont carefully observed how different materials burnt and concluded it involved the escape of a 'wild spirit' (spiritus silvestre). Van Helmont was the first person to understand that air is not a single substance but a mixture of substances, which he called gases. He discovered the gas carbon dioxide and showed that it is produced both in burning coal and the fermentation process of winemaking.

Burning is an irreversible reaction that requires fuel, oxygen, and a high enough temperature. This is described as the fire triangle, and all three have to be present for burning to occur. The reaction is capable of producing huge amounts of energy, which people have taken advantage of for thousands of years.

Fossil fuels are made from dead plants and animals that didn't decay because they were buried under water or mud with no oxygen. Fossil fuels are also known as hydrocarbons because they are made from molecules of carbon and hydrogen. When fossil fuels are burnt, the carbon and hydrogen react with oxygen in the air to produce carbon dioxide and water. The reaction releases the energy stored in the materials as heat and light. Carbon-based materials such as oil, wood, coal, natural gas, and paper readily burn in oxygen to produce gases which can be harmful and pollute the atmosphere.

Methane is a greenhouse gas

A major report published in 2019 by the Intergovernmental Panel on Climate Change (IPCC) called for a radical transformation of the food system. The report found that up to 37% of the world's total greenhouse gases come from the production of food and its refrigeration and transportation, and that about a third of the food is wasted. Methane emitted from farm animals, especially cows, was found to be one of the major contributors to climate change. Methane is a particular problem because its impact on global warming is much higher than carbon dioxide.

> Global methane levels have hit an all-time high after what appears to be a near-record yearly atmospheric increase in the potent greenhouse gas. . . . If confirmed later this year, it would be the second highest increase in methane levels in more than two decades. . . . Though methane remains in the atmosphere for only a few years, it is 28 times more powerful than carbon dioxide at trapping the sun's heat, and it poses an increasingly grave threat to efforts to tackle escalating global heating.
>
> (Independent Newspaper, April 2020)

Figure 5.5 Cows are sources of methane

Methane is made from carbon and hydrogen. It is produced naturally when bacteria decompose organic matter. Sources of methane come from mining fossil fuels, the digestive process of cows and other livestock, landfill sites, and natural leakages from the Earth. As the Earth warms up, more natural methane is being released into the atmosphere from the ocean floor, tropical wetlands, and from thawing permafrost in the Artic. Greater methane emissions mean more warming, which in turn releases more methane. This amounts to a dangerous feedback loop which can accelerate global warming. Already, methane is responsible for about 20% of the warming the Earth has experienced, and this is likely to increase if emissions are not reduced.

How digestion produces methane

The digestion process starts when the food is chewed in the mouth. It is then passed along the oesophagus and is broken down by chemicals in the stomach, which also kill any harmful microorganisms. The food passes to the small intestine, where nutrients are absorbed into the bloodstream and dispatched to the rest of the body. Finally, the waste passes into the large intestine, where trillions of bacteria get stuck into it. The food does not rush through the digestive system. Digestion is a slow process, starting with the stomach where it lingers about 5 hours, then it spends about 7 hours in the small intestine, and up to three days in the colon (large intestine). Times vary depending on the individual and the food that's been eaten.

Foods which are high in fibre, such as beans, peas, broccoli, and Brussels sprouts, are hardest to digest and likely to create the most 'gas'. Dietary fibre is made up of plant material (cellulose) that the digestive system cannot break down and absorb into the blood system. When it reaches the large intestine, microorganisms (good bacteria) feed on the fibrous food and in return for a meal they provide the body with health benefits. For example, they help control harmful bacteria, produce vital vitamins, and help support the immune system. A high-fibre diet also reduces the risk of heart disease, diabetes, and bowel cancer. There are trillions of bacteria inside our large intestines, and while they are feeding on the fibre, they produce methane and other gases which are expelled through the anus. The amount of methane produced by human digestion is small compared with the vast amount produced by cattle and other ruminants.

Carbon footprints

The carbon footprints of nations, industries, individual people, and animals provide ways of measuring the impact our activities have on the environment. Our carbon footprints are measured by the mass of greenhouse gases our activities are expected to produce each year, expressed in equivalent amounts of carbon dioxide. Research shows that a British citizen emits more CO2 in two weeks than some people in Africa do in a year.

The average person in the UK will have a greater carbon footprint by 12 January than some people in seven African nations will have in a year, research shows. By this month's second week, a British citizen will have overtaken a single person's annual emissions in Malawi, Ethiopia, Uganda, Madagascar, Guinea and Burkina Faso, according to Oxfam. It takes someone in the UK just five days to emit the same amount of carbon as someone in Rwanda does across a whole year . . .

(Independent Newspaper, Jan 2020)

The UK is ranked 36th in the world for its carbon footprint per head of population, and not surprisingly, 18 out of the 20 lowest carbon emitters were African countries. The six activities which make the biggest contribution to our carbon footprints in the UK are: heating our homes (9.7%), driving our cars (8.6%), use of electricity (8%), construction projects (6.7%), food and agriculture (6.6%), and air travel (5.9%).

Part 2: Working towards the big idea

This part provides ideas and activities which enable children to work towards understanding the big idea within a framework of good practice. Children's learning initially focuses on the evidence for climate change, which is both anecdotal and scientific in nature. They also learn about the causes of climate change, such as the burning of fossil fuels and the emission of methane from farm animals and landfill sites. Opportunities are provided for children to work on their understanding of burning as an irreversible process. They also learn about the digestive process, and compare the digestive systems of humans and ruminants. Learning directly related to the primary science curriculum includes changes of materials and digestion in animals and humans.

Children have opportunities to develop and use the following science and design technology skills:

- Work collaboratively towards common goals.
- Use different types of scientific enquiries, including data gathering and fair testing.
- Research using secondary sources.
- Generate, develop, model, and communicate ideas through discussion, sketches, and prototypes.
- Communicate outcomes of their research, enquiry, and design in different ways.
- Apply their learning in real-life contexts.

Health and safety

Follow the safety guidelines in ASE publication '*Be safe!*' when:

- planning the burning enquiry (Heating and burning p31);
- cooking high-fibre meals (Food and hygiene p15).

Exploring children's ideas

> Climate change has arrived and is accelerating faster than many scientists
> expected. It is more severe than anticipated, threatening natural ecosystems
> and the fate of humanity.
>
> Independent Newspaper, November 2019

Read the headline from the Independent Newspaper to the children. Do they agree with
what the headline says about climate change? Is there any evidence for climate change?
Have they noticed the climate changing?

Talking points: true, false, or not sure?

- Winters are getting colder and windier.
- Summers are becoming hotter and drier.
- Windy weather is more common, and the winds are stronger.
- It rains more often than it used to.
- Droughts have become more frequent and last longer.
- In the summer, thunderstorms are happening more frequently than in the past.

Groups try to reach agreement on their responses to the talking points. Encourage
children to justify their ideas. Groups come together to debate whether the climate is
changing. Talk together about whether opinion is the same as fact. What real evidence
do they have that the climate is changing?

Enquire! Anecdotal evidence for climate change

Children plan to survey their families and friends to discover whether they think the climate is changing. They can interview siblings, parents, grandparents, and family friends
to discover their opinions. Children plan the survey in two parts: Part 1 should record
quantitative data, which will require children to formulate questions with yes, no, or not
sure answers. Part 2 should have more open-ended questions to allow family and friends
to express and justify their opinions. Children record data in appropriate ways, including
the use of graphs. Back in school, children share, compare, discuss, analyse, and summarise their results in their groups. Groups then present their summaries to the rest of
the class. The class can debate whether they have collected reliable evidence for climate
change. What are the limitations of their evidence? Is the evidence only valid for the area
in which they live? Would a bigger sample of people provide more reliable evidence?

Research! Scientific evidence for climate change

Talk about how the scientific evidence for climate change is based on a huge amount
of weather data collected over many years. It is also based on data collected by orbiting satellites and climate models produced by super-computers, which can simulate the

Figure 5.6 Weather satellite

behaviour of the weather today and in the future. The evidence collected by scientists around the world clearly supports the belief that air temperatures are rising and the Earth's climate is changing.

Working in groups, children use information sources to review the scientific evidence for climate change. Introduce the children to organisations which provide reliable sources of information, such as NASA, ESA, The Met Office, The Royal Society, and the Natural History Museum. Talk about why children should choose reputable sources of information.

Conference! Evidence for climate change

Children organise a class conference to share and debate the evidence for the causes of climate change. Are we (people) responsible for the changes in the Earth's climate, or could there be other reasons that the climate is getting warmer? Groups use information sources to prepare an argument for or against man-made climate change. Groups then present their ideas to the conference. Children's ideas and opinions should be challenged with respect, and they should be encouraged to provide reasons for their ideas. Seek to reach agreement on whether there is strong evidence for man-made climate change. Organise a committee to write up and publish a report on the outcomes of the conference.

Information sources

Websites

- Arctic Climate Change | WWF Arctic (arcticwwf.org)
- Canada weather: Heat hits record 46.6°C as US north-west also sizzles – BBC News

- Conference of Youth (COY) | UNFCCC
- Climate Change: The evidence from Space (esa.int)
- Climate change resources for schools | WWF
- Evidence & Causes of Climate Change | Royal Society
- Evidence | Facts – Climate Change: Vital Signs of the Planet (nasa.gov)
- Latest data confirms 2020 concludes earth's warmest decade on record – NCAS

Working on scientific understanding

In this part, children work on their understanding of how the burning of fossil fuels contributes to climate change.

Earth Minute! Only ourselves to blame

Start by showing children the NASA Earth Minute video clip 'Usual Suspects' and discuss how we are responsible for climate change. Listen to children's ideas and address any major misconceptions.

Read the following extract to the children and ask them to explain why we need to stop burning fossil fuels. Listen to their responses and discuss how burning fossil fuels emits greenhouse gases. Talk about the greenhouse effect. Information and activities can be found in Chapter 4.

Figure 5.7 Air temperatures are rising to record levels

Humanity has just eight years to figure out how to get climate change under control before the future starts to look drastically worse – multiple-degree temperature increases, global sea-level rise, and increasingly disastrous wildfires, hurricanes, floods and droughts. Doing so will mean . . . humans will at some point have to stop burning oil, gas and coal.

Guardian Newspaper (Oct 2020)

Research! What are fossil fuels?

Working in groups, children use the web and other secondary sources to find out how fossil fuels are created from dead plants and animals. Groups present their findings to the class. Talk together about how fossil fuels store the Sun's energy.

Enquire! Burning fossil fuels

Start by asking children what they know about burning. Ask them to describe what happens to a material, such as paper, when it is burnt. Is it possible to reverse the process to get the paper back? Listen to children's ideas and address misconceptions.

Working in groups, children plan an enquiry to observe what happens to different types of materials when they burn. In a well-ventilated room they can burn small pieces of paper, card, wood, fabrics, and foods such as nuts (be aware of allergies). Use sand

Figure 5.8 Open pit coal mine

Figure 5.9 Burning produces gases

trays and safety candles, such as tea lights. Use fireproof tongs or wooden clothes pegs fixed to the end of a handle, to hold materials over the candle flame. Make sure children do not breathe in any fumes when carrying out the experiments. You may want the children to wear face masks and protective glasses, and of course warn them about the dangers of fire. Refer to the ASE publication '*Be Safe!*'

To record their observations, children take photographs before, during, and after burning. They should also measure the mass of each sample before and after burning. Groups present and compare their results with the rest of the class. Challenge them to explain why the fuels weigh less after they are burnt. Where has all the material gone? Talk together about the children's ideas and point out how new materials are formed, such as carbon dioxide and water which escape into the air. Introduce children to the fire triangle. Describe burning as an irreversible process that requires fuel, oxygen, and a high enough temperature.

Focus children's attention on burning fossil fuels. Remind them that fossil fuels are made from dead plants and animals, and how they store energy. Describe burning as a process which releases the energy stored in the fossil fuels. Explain that fossil fuels (hydrocarbons) are made from hydrogen and carbon and when they are burnt, the carbon and the hydrogen react with oxygen in the air to produce carbon dioxide and water (H_2O). The reaction produces heat and light energy. Link these ideas with other curriculum work on changing materials.

Natural gas

Ask children how they heat their homes. Talk about how most people burn natural gas to heat their water and their heating systems. Use burning natural gas as an example of an irreversible process involving a chemical change. Natural gas is mainly methane, made up of carbon and hydrogen. When burnt in oxygen, it produces carbon dioxide and water and releases large amounts of heat energy.

Methane + oxygen + high temperature → carbon dioxide + water + energy.

Point out how reducing our carbon footprints means using low carbon energy resources to heat and light our homes. Examples of low carbon resources can be found in Chapter 8.

Art! The science behind global warming

Show and discuss NASA's Earth Minute video, *Gas Problem*. Working in groups, children produce their own cartoon presentation entitled, *The Science behind global warming*. The cartoons should depict how carbon dioxide emissions are produced and how they increase the greenhouse gases in the atmosphere. Groups use their cartoons to provide a one-minute poster presentation about how burning fossil fuels contributes to climate change.

Story-telling! Life without fossil fuels

It was 2020 when the article in the Guardian Newspaper declared that we have only eight years to get climate change under control to avoid disaster, and to do so we would have to stop burning fossil fuels. A number of years has gone by already, and most of the energy we use still comes from fossil fuels.

Ask children to imagine what life would be like if fossil fuels had never been discovered. They should tell their story of 'Life without fossil fuels' in the form of a diary, in which they record their activities over a seven-day period. The diary should include the activities of each member of their family at home, school, and at work. Diary entries should refer to travel, food and cooking, clothes, communication, occupations, shopping, and all the other things they do now on a daily basis. Talk to the children as they are working on their diaries and ask them to justify their recordings. Children share and justify their ideas in groups. Bring the class together to decide whether life would be better or worse without technologies that burn fossil fuels. Children compare their lives today with what life was like for most people before the Industrial Revolution. Talk about how technologies that burn fossil fuels have improved our quality of life, and also highlight the problems they have caused. Do the advantages outweigh the disadvantages? Listen to children's ideas and talk about whether they think it is feasible to stop using fossil fuels. If we do stop, how will it affect our lives?

Information sources

Websites

- Earth Minute Videos | Explore – Climate Change: Vital Signs of the Planet (nasa.gov)
- Explainer: How and why fires burn | Science News for Students
- Climate change explained – GOV.UK (www.gov.uk)

- Climate change driving entire planet to dangerous 'tipping point' | National Geographic
- Climate change resources for schools | WWF
- Effects of climate change – Met Office
- Shaping our Future | WWF
- What are fossil fuels, and why are they such popular energy sources? – ABC News
- What is climate change and why does it matter? | Natural History Museum (nhm.ac.uk)
- WWF_Climate_Explainer.pdf

The bigger picture

In this part, children explore how farm animals contribute to climate change, and consider how farming practices need to change.

Burping! Methane is a major greenhouse gas

Children may be surprised to learn that natural emissions of greenhouse gases from farm animals contribute to climate change. Ask them whether they think burping can harm the planet. Listen to their ideas and talk about how cows, goats, and sheep emit a gas called methane when they burp. Explain methane is made from carbon and hydrogen and, like carbon dioxide, it is a greenhouse gas that helps warm up the planet. Point out that methane is already responsible for about 20% of the warming of the Earth, and this is likely to increase if emissions are not reduced.

Explore! The digestive system

Ask children what they know about the causes of burping. Is it caused by what they eat, or is it because they talk too much?! Working in groups, children list and discuss the reasons why they burp. Ask them to list the top ten foods which give them 'wind'. Groups come together to share their ideas and classify the types of food which are most likely to cause flatulence and belching. Do vegetables or meat give them wind? Do some vegetables create more wind than other types of food?

Ask children to describe what happens to their food after they put it in their mouths. Working collaboratively, children draw full-sized outlines of their body shape and draw in the major organs. This can be done using chalk on the playground or using large sheets of paper on the floor of the school hall. Take photographs to record their chalk drawings. Children come together to compare their pictures and explain what they know about the digestive system. Groups trace the path the food takes in their digestive system. Probe children's understanding and address misconceptions. Encourage children to speculate about why some foods cause burping and flatulence. Draw their attention to high-fibre foods, which are difficult to digest.

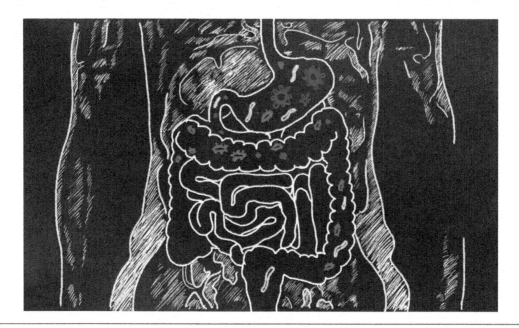

Figure 5.10 Human digestive system

Talking points: true, false, or not sure?

- I digest my food so my body can use it to keep healthy.
- After it is digested, my blood transports the food to all parts of my body.
- My mouth is not part of my digestive system.
- Most of my food is digested in my stomach.
- I digest my food so it will travel faster through my system.
- I waste a lot of food when I have a poo.
- My small intestine digests most of my food.
- Chemical reactions go on inside my digestive system.
- There are trillions of microorganisms feeding on the food inside my digestive system.
- Bad food gives me gas (wind).

Children work in groups to respond to the talking points. Listen to their ideas and address misconceptions. Focus their attention on what digestion means and what goes on in different parts of the digestive system.

Model! The digestive system

Children use the web and other secondary sources to find out what goes on in each part of their digestive system. They can model through role-play or make their own tabard models using card or fabric to help them present their ideas.

You can also involve the whole class in role-play. You will need a large space for this activity. Tell children they are going to role-play the digestive system. Some children will act the role of the mouth, others form a tunnel to represent the oesophagus, others link hands in a ring to form the stomach, and others need to work out how to form the large and small intestines. Use large pieces of foam which can be squashed in different parts of the system to present the digestive process. Help children narrate the process as the food (foam) moves through the digestive system.

Talk about foods which are high in fibre, such as beans, peas, broccoli and Brussels sprouts, being hardest to digest and likely to create the most 'gas'. Make the point that there are trillions of bacteria inside our large intestines, and while they are feeding on the fibre, they produce methane and other gases which are expelled through the anus. Talk about the health benefits of eating a balanced, high-fibre diet.

Explore! High-fibre meals

The NHS recommends that children aged from 6 to 11 years should eat about 20g of fibre per day. Talk about how fibre is mainly found in cereals, fruit, and vegetables. Remind children why fibre is an important part of their diet. Working in small groups, children use information sources to discover the amount of fibre in different types of food products. They use the information to plan meals for a day which provide 20g of fibre. Meals should include breakfast, playtime snack, lunch, after school snack, and dinner in the evening. Groups compare their choice of food with what they usually eat.

As a treat, children choose the ingredients for a high-fibre pizza that they cook and eat in the school. Allow each group to choose their own ingredients and to make their own pizza. Children must work out how much fibre their pizza will provide. If you don't have cooking facilities in your school, children can make high-fibre sandwiches or paninis. Refer to ASE *Be Safe* booklet for health and safety advice, and be aware of dietary requirements for your pupils.

Explore! Ruminants

Start by asking children why cows and sheep produce a lot more methane than people. Why do dogs and cats not produce as much methane? Compare what cows and sheep eat with what the children and their pets eat. Ask them to speculate about how much grass a cow or sheep eats each day. Working in groups, children use the web and other secondary sources to compare their digestive systems with those of cows, dogs, and cats. Each group creates a display highlighting similarities and differences in the digestive systems. Can they predict the digestive system of an animal from what it eats? Ask them to sketch the digestive system of a sheep, a camel, and a deer.

Fact! Methane is 23% more powerful than carbon dioxide

Draw children's attention to the fact that methane accounts for 14% of the greenhouse gases emitted in the atmosphere. Point out that it is a much more powerful greenhouse gas than carbon dioxide, and to get climate change under control we need to reduce the

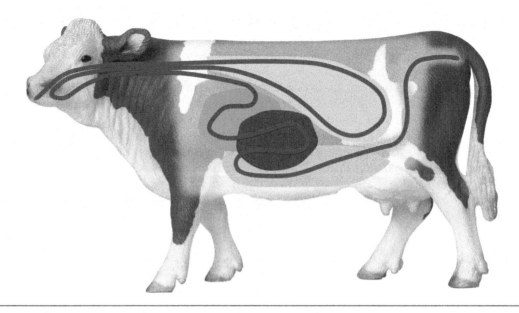

Figure 5.11 A cow's digestive system

emissions, especially those due to livestock. Working in groups, children plan a reform of farming practices to reduce methane emissions. Provide a political context for the work, in which the groups represent the Department of Agriculture and have been tasked by the Prime Minister to present their reform plans in time for the next general election.

Things for groups to consider include:

1. How the reforms will affect the diets of the electorate, and also the prices of food.
2. How the electorate are likely to respond to the reforms.
3. How the reforms are likely to impact the farming industry, including changes that need to be made.
4. How the farmers are likely to respond to the reforms. Will the reforms put some farmers out of business?

Groups present their reforms to a full Downing St cabinet meeting. Members of the cabinet (the class) raise questions concerning the feasibility of the reforms and vote whether they should be accepted. Conclude by talking about whether the children would be prepared to eat less red meat and cheese, and instead eat more vegetables and other non-meat products to reduce methane emissions.

Information sources

Websites

- Burp by Burp, Fighting Emissions from Cows (nationalgeographic.com)
- High-fibre diet for children (wsh.nhs.uk)

- Methane facts and information (nationalgeographic.com)
- Methane from cows is hastening climate change: can these drugs stop them burping? | World Economic Forum
- Methane levels at all-time high after near-record increase in gas 28 times more potent than carbon dioxide | The Independent
- Ruminant Animals: Full List and Fun Facts (animalwised.com)
- WWF Footprint Calculator

Books

- Loxley, P., Dawes, L., Nicholls, L., and Dore, B. (2018) *Teaching Primary Science*. Abingdon: Routledge.
- Loxley, P. (2018) *Practical Ideas for Teaching Primary Science*. Abingdon: Routledge.

CHAPTER 6

IMPACT OF CLIMATE CRISIS ON OUR LIVES

Big idea: *Climate change is accelerating faster than expected and is threatening natural ecosystems and the fate of humanity.*

   This chapter provides opportunities for children to explore the effect the climate crisis is having on the weather, and its impact on the lives of people in different parts of the world. Part 1 sets the context for children's learning by providing media accounts of the devastation caused by extreme weather events, such as flash flooding, droughts, and heat waves. The subject knowledge also shines a light on the plight of the developing world, and exposes how the crisis is hitting the poorest in the world the hardest. Part 2 sets out models of good practice which provide ideas and activities which teachers can use to organise children's learning of the big idea. The ideas presented provide real-life contexts to extend and enrich the primary science and geography curricula.

The subject knowledge topics include:

- Rising sea levels
- Nuisance flooding
- Flash flooding around the world
- Wildfires
- Adapting to climate change
- Conflict between people and wildlife
- Food security and safety
- Conflict and migration

Part 1: Subject knowledge

In 2019, dozens of scientists collaborated to send this message about the dangers of climate change:

DOI: 10.4324/9781003166276-6

Climate change has arrived and is accelerating faster than many scientists expected. It is more severe than anticipated, threatening natural ecosystems and the fate of humanity. Researchers say they have a moral obligation to clearly warn humanity of any catastrophic threat and tell it like it is. Clearly and unequivocally planet Earth is facing a climate emergency.

(BioScience, 2019)

A further 11,000 scientists from 153 nations endorsed the statement, warning that climate change will bring untold suffering for large populations of people around the world and the mass extinction of wildlife. The crisis is due to the effects of human activity on our planet's weather and climate systems, and is set to get worse as we continue to pump vast amounts of greenhouse gases into the atmosphere.

Rising sea levels

Global warming is melting ice worldwide, especially in the Arctic and Antarctic regions. Greenland and the Antarctic are covered by huge amounts of land ice which is decreasing rapidly. As the ice melts it flows into the oceans, raising sea levels. Global sea levels are rising faster each year as increasing temperatures melt more ice. Oceans are also expanding due to global warming, which together with melting ice are causing average sea levels to rise by 3.2 mm a year. This may not seem like a lot, but scientists predict that by the end of the century the global sea level will have risen by 30 cm, and in the worst-case scenario, could rise by 2.5 metres above the level at the beginning of the century.

As sea levels rise, the risk of flooding in coastal towns and cities becomes greater. About 40% of people around the world live within 100 km of the coastline and are at risk of flooding if sea levels continue to rise. Rising sea levels also add to the destructive power of hurricanes and storms by enabling storm surges to push further inland. Hurricanes can be devastating, causing huge amounts of damage and substantial loss of life. More information on hurricanes can be found in Chapter 3.

Nuisance flooding

Higher sea levels also mean more frequent flooding due to high tides. This can be called nuisance flooding, but for those people affected, the trouble and expense it can cause amount to much more than just a nuisance!

Over recent years, parts of the UK have been hit with high tides and flooding due to exceptional weather. Seaside towns have been subject to massive tidal surges, with buildings and infrastructure taking a pounding from the waves. Flooding along the UK's coastline is frequent and widespread, especially in the Southwest where waves often breach sea defences, flood roads, and cause distress to local habitants. The following announcement is typical of the regular flood warnings put out by the Environment Agency:

Waves are forecast to overtop sea defences with sea spray expected as a result of high tides and strong winds for tomorrow morning and evening

Figure 6.1 Waves battering Brighton Marina, UK

tides. High water is forecast at 6:30am on Sunday morning and 7:30pm on Sunday evening. The wind strength is Force 7 from the south west. Flooding to roads is expected and may apply two to four hours either side of the high tides. We are closely monitoring the situation. Please stay away from large waves and be careful along beaches, promenades and coastal footpaths and roads.

(Bridport News, Nov 2020)

Flash flooding in the UK

The frequency and intensity of heavy rainfall is increasing in many areas of the world, including the UK. Heavy rainfall can overwhelm drainage systems or burst riverbanks, causing flash flooding in towns and cities. Due to flash flooding, roads can become like rivers, flooding homes and carrying away cars.

Homes have been damaged, roads destroyed and cars left partially-submerged under water due to flash flooding in Somerset. People have shared pictures of cars stranded, homes flooded and roads blocked with debris. Chard, which is one of the worst-hit areas, saw more than a month's worth of rain fall in just three hours – turning roads into rivers. The average June rainfall for Chard is 50mm but it experienced 64.2mm

Figure 6.2 Flooding in southwest England

in three hours and 96.8mm in a 24-hour period. Emergency shelters have been set up to help people affected and two people in Somerset have been rescued by boat and taken to dry land after getting stuck in floodwater.

(ITV News, June 2021)

Winters in 2013/14 and 2015/16 were the wettest ever recorded in the UK, causing widespread flooding, power cuts, and major disruptions to transport. The worst-affected areas were the Southwest and the Thames Valley in the Southeast. A study by the Met Office has shown that extreme winter rainfall is now about 7 times more likely due to climate change. Scientific studies suggest that climate change has increased the risks of floods in parts of the UK by at least 20%, and perhaps as much as 90%.

Flash flooding around the world

The extracts from news reports create a picture of the havoc flash flooding has brought to communities around the world in recent years. The devastation includes loss of life and the destruction of homes, transport systems, and agriculture.

In 2021, flooding in Europe was amongst the worst experienced, with over 200 people losing their lives. Flooding due to heavy rains started in the UK, and spread to Austria, Belgium, Croatia, Germany, Luxembourg, the Netherlands, and Switzerland. In the same year, flash flooding brought havoc to many parts of India, Africa, Asia, and Central

America. Parts of central China experienced their heaviest rainfall on record, which affected 9.3 million people. Over 300 people lost their lives, and over a million people had to be relocated.

As the news reports show, flooding brings chaos and devastation to people's lives. If the climate crisis is not addressed then flooding is likely to get worse, with even more disastrous consequences.

Flash flooding news reports

Europe

> The death toll from the heavy flooding that swept through parts of Western Europe has passed 150, as rescuers continue to search for the missing. The vast majority of deaths have occurred in Germany, while media reports suggest at least 27 people have died in Belgium. The Netherlands remains on high alert as overflowing rivers threatened towns and villages throughout the southern province of Limburg. Luxembourg and France has also been affected by flooding, which erupted amid relentless rain and storms. Homes have been covered in water and brought down in some cases and vehicles carried away by streams after rivers and reservoirs burst their banks.
>
> Independent Newspaper, July 2021

Figure 6.3 Flooding in Germany (2021)

Africa

South Sudan flooding affects more than 600,000. Torrential rains cause rivers to overflow, deluging homes and farms in eight of the country's 10 states, UN agency says. Schools, homes, health facilities and water sources were inundated, impacting people's access to basic services. Physical access remained a major challenge for humanitarian organizations to assess and respond to the needs of flood-affected people. Some families have been able to flee to the capital, Juba, while others have set up makeshift camps along highways, grabbing what few possessions they could from the ruins of their flimsy thatched huts.

(Aljazeera, October 2021)

Asia

China is facing the daunting challenges of climate change after modernizing at a time when its leaders favored economic growth over climate resiliency, making many of its cities ill-equipped to absorb water from torrential downpours. Though flooding is a complex problem with many causes, climate change is causing heavier rainfall in many storms. In early August, the government said 302 people had died in Henan Province from flooding since mid-July, including 14 who died in a subway tunnel that rapidly flooded in Zhengzhou. There were similarly heavy rains last summer, killing hundreds and causing billions in economic losses.

The New York Times August 2021

Figure 6.4 Flooding in Kerala, India

Central America

Storm Eta has unleashed torrential rains, and catastrophic landslides and flooding in Central America, killing scores of people, displacing more than 300,000, and turning city streets into raging torrents. At least 50 people died in Guatemala, including 25 who were killed in a landslide in the village of Quejá, according to the country's president, Alejandro Giammattei. He also told local radio that 60% of the eastern city of Puerto Barrios was flooded and 48 more hours of rain were expected. Authorities reported nearly 100 homes damaged by flooding and landslides in Guatemala. Footage posted on social media showed canoes navigating through the flooded streets of the Honduran city of San Pedro Sula, where scores of people perched on roofs, pleading to be rescued.

(Guardian Newspaper, Nov 2020)

Wildfires

It is not only flooding that devastates people's lives. As I write, wildfires are ripping through the Greek island of Evia. The fires have destroyed a large part of the island, with more than 2,000 people being evacuated to the mainland. Fires are also raging in other parts of Greece due to the record summer temperatures:

In Greece, Eleni Myrivili, who was appointed Athens' first chief heat officer in July, described "apocalyptic" scenes after houses and villages burned down as a result of wildfires in the north-east of the Greek capital amid a protracted heatwave. The most intense days for the fires were Tuesday and Wednesday as temperatures reached 45C.

(Guardian Newspaper, August 2021)

Due to climate change, heatwaves are becoming more intense and more frequent in all parts of the world, with July 2021 being the hottest month ever recorded on Earth. Throughout the summer of 2021, countries in Europe and North America experienced record temperatures, with many of them battling devastating wildfires as the regions suffered their worst heatwaves in decades. Major wildfires were recorded in Algeria, South Africa, India, Russia, Turkey, Greece, Italy (Sardinia, Sicily, and Calabria), Cyprus, Canada, Argentina, Australia, and the USA. In the USA, there were major fires in eight states, with 311 fires in the first four months of 2021 in Arizona, compared to 127 in the same period in 2020. In central and southern regions of Italy, the number of large wildfires was triple the yearly average, while at the same time, regions in the north were plagued by severe flooding. Sardinia was particularly hard-hit by one of the largest wildfires in living memory:

Wildfires Ravage Sardinia in 'a Disaster without Precedent'

A 25-mile swath of vegetation, farms and villages is hit by one of the largest wildfires in decades, devastating the Italian tourist destination. About 1,000 residents and tourists have been evacuated from areas of western Sardinia that were ravaged by wildfires over the weekend, with forests, pastures and villages on the Italian island engulfed in flames. "It is a disaster without precedent," said the region's governor, Christian Solinas, invoking a state of emergency on Sunday.

(The New York Times, August 2021)

Adapting to climate change

By adapting to the impacts of the climate crisis, we can make ourselves and the places where we live less vulnerable. For example, to protect against more frequent flooding due to rises in sea levels, communities might build seawalls or build new houses on higher ground.

The effects of the climate crisis are hitting many of the world's poorest people the hardest, and making their lives even worse. Flooding and other natural disasters destroy harvests and homes, creating devastation from which people living in poverty find it hard to recover.

> People living in poverty suffer most from the effects of flooding. Poverty makes it more difficult for people to cope with flooding and recover from the effects as they have less money and support to rebuild their homes and buildings

(Practical Action website)

Flooding is widespread in developing countries and is a major problem in some regions. For example, the 7,000 islands that make up the Philippines are particularly vulnerable to flooding, sometimes resulting in entire communities being swept away. Millions of children in the Philippines live in poverty, and it is often these children who are most affected by flooding and other natural disasters.

Practical Action and ActionAid are charities that help people in the developing world to find solutions to their problems, many of which are made worse by the climate crisis. If people are prepared for flooding, they can reduce the chaos the floods bring to their lives, and can recover from the damage more quickly. These charities work with communities to help them prepare for flooding and adapt to the effects of climate change.

Conflict between people and wildlife

In Africa, large numbers of big mammals, including several hundred thousand wild elephants and more than 20,000 lions, still roam freely in some regions. The people who live in these regions have to cope with the consequences, which include destruction of crops and livestock, competition for grazing and water, increased risk of livestock diseases, loss of sleep due to protecting crops at night, and even danger to their lives. As global warming continues, the conflict between people and wildlife is likely to get worse as droughts force animals to search for food and water ever closer to human settlements.

The African elephant is already in decline due to poaching and the loss of habitats due to the development of farms, settlements, and roads. Areas of land, such as the Amboseli National Park, have been set aside to protect what is left of the elephant's habitat. However, elephants traditionally roam long distances in search of food and often

Figure 6.5 Elephant roaming in African village

stray outside the boundaries of the protected areas onto land occupied by people, which can lead to conflict. Communities that live near nature reserves are often poor and rely on their farms to survive. Damage to their crops caused by elephants and other wildlife can threaten their ability to feed themselves.

As evidenced by the plight of the Arctic polar bears described in the next chapter, human-animal conflict is a growing problem all around the world due to the unrelenting destruction of wildlife habitats, made worse by climate change.

Food security and safety

High temperatures, extreme weather, flooding, and droughts can damage farmland, making it more difficult to grow crops. Due to the climate crisis, the production of major food crops such as wheat, rice, and maize are likely to be adversely affected. As a result, the supply of food around the world will be less certain, with shortages leading to higher prices, less-healthy diets, greater levels of malnutrition, and increased famine, particularly in the developing world.

According to the World Health Organisation (WHO), the climate crisis is also likely to have considerable impact on people's health due to increased contamination of food and water by harmful bacteria, viruses, and fungi. The sensitivity of germs to climate factors suggests that the climate crisis can lead to a greater number of dangerous food-borne diseases, especially regarding toxin-producing algae affecting seafood. Again, the people likely to be most affected are those in developing countries.

Conflict and migration

The climate crisis is predicted to make existing difficulties worse, especially problems associated with crop failure and lack of food and shelter. This can cause conflict over resources, leading to civil unrest or perhaps even full-scale war. Today, the world experiences large-scale migration of millions of desperate people from developing countries who are fleeing conflict and poverty. Governments in the developed world are struggling to cope with the large numbers who are seeking asylum. If the climate crisis continues to escalate, it is predicted that the number of asylum seekers will dramatically increase in future years.

> As their land fails them, hundreds of millions of people from Central America to Sudan to the Mekong Delta will be forced to choose between flight or death. The result will almost certainly be the greatest wave of global migration the world has ever seen.
>
> (The New York Times Magazine, 2020)

People are already on the move. In Southeast Asia, where monsoon rains are becoming increasingly unpredictable, more than eight million people have moved towards the Middle East, Europe, and North America. Also, in parts of Africa, millions of rural people are moving towards the coasts and cities amidst drought and widespread crop failures. Scientists predict that the climate crisis will increase the problems for many farmers in the developing world, and suggest that mass migration could result in the remapping of the world's populations.

Figure 6.6 Immigrants trying to enter Europe

Part 2: Working towards the big idea

This part provides ideas and activities which enable children to work towards under-standing the big idea within a framework of good practice. Learning starts with explor-ing children's experience of storms and flooding, and through enquiry and role-play they develop their understanding of the use of flood defences to protect property. Sci-entific enquiry and research activities enable children to explore reasons why global warming is causing more rainfall and causing sea levels to rise, both of which can lead to flooding. By exploring the bigger picture, children are able to discover why the climate crisis is likely to hit the poorest people in the world the hardest, and how it is helping to fuel human-animal conflict.

Children have opportunities to develop and use the following science and design technology skills:

- Work collaboratively towards common goals.
- Use different types of scientific enquiries, including data gathering and fair testing.
- Research using secondary sources.
- Generate, develop, model, and communicate ideas through discussion, sketches, and prototypes.
- Communicate outcomes of their research and enquiry in different ways.
- Apply their learning in real-life contexts.

Exploring children's ideas

Share the following weather warning, or a more recent report of a major weather inci-dent, with the children:

> A major incident has been declared in South Yorkshire as Storm Christoph is set to bring widespread flooding to parts of England . . . . The Met Office issued an amber weather warning for rain in Yorkshire and the Humber, the Northwest, East Midlands and the east of England. The Environment Agency said the combination of heavy rain and snowmelt created a "volatile situation". Sandbags were laid in at-risk areas, with up to 70mm (2.75in) of rain due.
>
> (BBC News online Jan 2021)

Listen to children's experiences of storms, flooding, and other extreme weather. Show them videos of the destructive effects of flooding in the UK. Examples can be found on the National Geographic website. Groups create a poster using headlines and images collected from online newspaper reports about extreme weather events in the UK. Use the posters to create a classroom display. Children continue exploring the web to find evidence of flash flooding in the UK. What damage has it caused? Why is flash flooding so dangerous?

Higher and higher!

Due to heavy rainfall in February 2020, Shrewsbury, in Shropshire (UK), was badly affected by flooding when the River Severn rose by 4.85 metres, its highest level in 20 years. The town centre was flooded, with many homes and businesses flooded out. Measure the height of the classroom to help children appreciate how high the flood water rose. Most classrooms would be less than 3 metres high. Talk about whether the school has any buildings which are over 4.85 metres high. Chalk a line 4.8 metres long in the playground. Invite children to lie next to the line to see how far the flood water would have risen above their heads. Also, mark the height of the classroom on the line to make children aware of how high the water rose. Challenge groups to use information sources to discover rivers around the world which have risen to higher levels. Children explain where the rivers are located, and the problems caused by the subsequent flooding. Mark each discovery on a world map.

Story-telling! Local community hit hard by flash flooding

Ask children to imagine they were journalists working at the time of the flood for the local Shrewsbury newspaper, the *Shropshire Star*. Children use information sources and their imaginations to write a newspaper article about the impact of the flood on the local community. Although the story is fiction, the events should be based on the reality of what flooding can do to a community. Encourage children to justify the plausibility of events described in their article.

Street Art! Ignoring the climate crisis

Isaac Cordal is a unique street-art artist whose works shine a critical light on how absurd and precarious our behaviour can be, especially with regard to the natural world. His works involve sculptures of 'little people' set in urban landscapes. The figures are placed in locations which invite us to empathise with their tenuous situations, as the world blindly ignores the future consequences of the climate crisis. Children explore Cordal's work on the web, especially those associated with flooding and climate change, such as the installations entitled *Follow the leaders* and *Waiting for climate change*. Following in Cordal's footsteps, children make their own thought-provoking installations featuring 'little people', created to send alarming messages about our future if we continue to ignore the climate crisis. Children make their figures out of a suitable material, such as Plasticine or clay, and create their installations in appropriate parts of the school. Alternatively, they could create large-scale paintings which convey similar messages. Children add captions to their displays or paintings intended to spark the viewer's imagination.

Figure 6.7 'Waiting for climate change' by Isaac Cordal

Figure 6.8 Sandbag barrier

Model! Flood defences

During flooding, people often build barriers with sandbags and other materials to pre-vent the water flooding into their homes through the doors. Ask children to think of what they would do to protect their homes from flooding.

Working in groups, children try out their ideas by building suitable models. For exam-ple, if they choose to use sandbags, they can build their models using sandwich bags filled with sand or other similar material. Encourage children to explore the best way to build the barrier. Which shape is the strongest? They can test their models outside using a watering can or a hosepipe to create a flood.

Adapting to flooding problems

Start this activity by assessing the school's flood risk. Has the school ever been flooded? Is it built close to a river, on low-lying land, or on a flood plain? Listen to children's experi-ences of flooding. Working in groups, children use information sources to discover areas of the UK that are most prone to flooding. Children record the areas on a giant map of the UK. Talk together about the reasons why the areas are at risk of flooding.

Ask children to imagine that they lived in an area where they had been flooded out of their homes more than once in the last five years. Because of the risk of flooding, it would be almost impossible to insure their homes, and they probably wouldn't be able to sell them. Talk about the problems people who live in these areas face and how the climate crisis is likely to make things worse in the future. Brainstorm what the local residents could do to adapt to the flooding problem. This is the background to the role-play activity.

Role-play! Resilient Residents

A number of residents band together to do something about flooding. Before they petition the council, the residents thrash out an argument to persuade the council to do something about the flooding. Residents (children) work in groups to prepare their argument. The argument should include the problems flooding has caused over the last five years, based on real accounts reported in local and national media. The argument should also include reasons why the situation is likely to get worse in the future, based on climate change predictions from reliable sources. Groups come together to share their arguments and decide what they need to write to the council. A letter can be pre-pared and displayed.

The council responds to the letter by asking local contractors to tender plans for installing flood defences. Plans should include:

1. A map of the local area where the flooding takes place, with the position of the flood defences clearly marked;
2. Drawings and models of the defences that will be constructed.

Each group represents a different contractor and presents its plans to the council (the class). The council take a vote on the plans to choose which ones are likely to be most effective.

Draw children's attention to a study by the Met Office which shows that extreme winter rainfall is now seven times more likely due to the climate crisis, and consequently risks of flooding are 20% to 90% more likely, depending on where you live. Encourage children to speculate about and debate the likely future flooding problems if global warming continues. What do they suggest should be done?

STEM ambassador

Invite a STEM ambassador, or local council representative, who specialises in civil engineering projects to your school, and ask him/her to talk to the children about the increased risk of flooding due to the climate crisis. Children prepare questions about their own area to discover potential flood problems, and to find out what can be done to solve them.

Information sources

Websites

- Adapting to Climate Change | UCAR Center for Science Education
- Climate crisis: 11,000 scientists warn of 'untold suffering' | Climate crisis | The Guardian
- Earth's hottest month was record hot in 2021 | NOAA Climate.gov
- Flood warnings for England – GOV.UK (flood-warning-information.service.gov.uk)
- Floods – facts and information (nationalgeographic.com)
- Flooding in China kills 21, as thousands escape to shelters. – The New York Times (nytimes.com)
- Global climate emergency: 11,000 scientists from across world unite to issue unprecedented declaration | The Independent | The Independent
- Storm Christoph: Flood warnings in parts of England – BBC News
- South Sudan flooding affects more than 600,000: UN | Floods News | Al-Jazeera
- What causes flash floods? – Met Office
- Works – Isaac Cordal (cementeclipses.com)

Working on scientific understanding

In this part, children work on their understanding of the science behind the climate crisis. They start by exploring the reasons global warming can cause wetter weather.

Enquire! How warming creates wetter weather

Working in groups, children explore the impact of a warmer climate on rainfall using a simple water cycle model made from resealable sandwich bags. This model is adapted from ideas presented on the WWF website.

Explain that the air inside the sandwich bag represents the atmosphere. Fill a bag full of air by dragging through the air with the bag open. Then seal the air inside. This is the control model. Now take another bag, fill it with air, and add a measured amount of water. Mark the level of water on the outside of the bag. The water represents surface water, which evaporates to make rain. Place both models in a warm area of the classroom and observe what happens. Children should see drops of water forming on the sides and towards the top of the bag with the water in it. Some of the drops fall back into the water, modelling precipitation. To investigate the effect warming has on 'rainfall', groups can use a lamp (Sun) to heat the air and water inside the bag. Groups turn off the lamp and observe the impact that warming has on the 'rainfall'.

Children compare the 'rainfall' in each case with the control experiment. Talk about the science. Discuss how warmer air holds more water vapour. In fact, the amount of moisture that can be held in air grows very rapidly as temperatures increase. Therefore, we can expect the air to get moister (humid) as the Earth warms and as more water evaporates from the oceans. This may cause more frequent and intense rainfall events, which lead to increased risk of flooding.

Enquire! How rising sea levels can cause flooding

Talk about rising sea levels as another major cause of flooding. Start by talking about how rising temperatures in the Arctic regions are causing massive amounts of ice to melt. Much of this extra water flows into oceans, causing sea levels to rise. Also, the oceans are becoming warmer as they absorb the heat trapped by greenhouse gases in the Earth's atmosphere. As sea water gets warmer it expands, causing a further rise in sea levels.

Figure 6.9 Melting sea ice

In this activity, children use model icebergs to discover whether melting icebergs are responsible for rising sea levels. Make models of icebergs using ice balloons. Make ice balloons by filling balloons full of water and leaving them in a freezer until the water becomes frozen. Children compare the volume of their balloons before and after freezing. Strip off the rubber to create a model iceberg. Float the iceberg in warm water and mark the level of the water in the container before the icebergs start to melt. As the iceberg melts, children record any changes in the water level. Is it likely that melting sea ice causes sea levels to rise? Discuss how an iceberg floats in water. Much of it floats beneath the surface. Use an ice balloon to demonstrate. Remind children that when ice freezes its volume increases, and when it melts the volume of the water reduces back again. So, when an iceberg melts its volume reduces and fits into the space taken up by that part of the iceberg beneath the water. Contrary to what many people think, this means melting sea ice does not cause the water level to rise. It is the vast amounts of extra water from melting land ice that cause rises in sea levels.

Model! Rising sea levels

Children can explore the effect melting land ice has on sea levels by creating a model of the Antarctic shoreline in a large bowl. The model is constructed from small rocks to represent the land, surrounded by water which represents the sea. Ice cubes are piled on the land to represent glaciers and other land ice. Groups mark the water level before and after the ice melts, and observe and record the rise in 'sea level'. Children plan their own experiments to explore how rises in water temperature impact the sea level. Discuss the outcomes of the children's investigations and talk about how global warming is causing sea levels to rise.

Figure 6.10 Melting land ice

Case-study! Communities most affected by rising sea levels

Working in groups, children use information sources to explore areas of the world which are most prone to rising sea levels. Point out that over 300 million people currently live in areas which are prone to flooding due to rising seas levels, many of whom live on low-lying islands. Each group identifies and maps vulnerable communities in different parts of the world, and chooses two of them to case-study. Case-studies should include at least one island community.

Case-studies should focus on:

- The geography of the countries
- Change in weather patterns due to global warming
- The effects rising sea levels are having or likely to have on the communities
- What can be done to adapt to the impact of rising sea levels

Groups come together to share their findings and create a large-scale map of the world showing the areas most exposed to flooding due to rising sea levels. Talk about how the effects of the climate crisis are hitting many of the world's poorest people the hardest.

Information sources

Websites

- Beat the flood – Practical Action
- Climate change and poverty | ActionAid UK
- Climate Change: Global Sea Level | NOAA Climate.gov
- Dramatic decline in sea ice levels in Antarctica | 7.30 – Bing video
- Education resources – Practical Action
- Is sea level rising? (noaa.gov)
- Melting glaciers will dominate sea-level rise | New Scientist

The bigger picture

In this part, children examine the impact of the climate crisis on communities in different areas of the world. Learning starts with children examining the devastation wildfires can cause to communities and wildlife in fire-prone areas of the world. They are then asked to put themselves in the place of people who live in the areas of Eastern Australia that are prone to bushfires. Children then go on to examine the impact of the climate crisis on some of the world's poorest people, and also explore possible solutions to a human-animal conflict problem.

Research! Wildfires

Talk about how wildfires around the world are becoming more frequent and more destructive than ever before, due to extreme hot weather caused by climate change increasing the intensity and size of the fires. In 2021, major wildfires were recorded in Africa, Asia, Europe, North and South America, and Australia. More details can be found in Part 1.

Divide the class into 6 groups and assign each group a continent to research on the web. Ask each group to discover the areas of the continent which are most prone to wildfires and to document the most recent fires. Children should document the scale of the destruction inflicted by the fires on communities and wildlife. Groups come together to present and discuss their findings, and to record the approximate location of the wildfires on a large-scale map of the world.

Story-telling! Bushfires in Australia

Focus children's attention on wildfires in Australia. Talk about how in recent years Australia has experienced some of the worst bushfires in its recorded history. For example, in November 2019, major bushfires started in New South Wales, with others springing up in Victoria, Western Australia, South Australia, and the Australian Capital Territory. Millions of hectares of bush were burnt, with thousands of properties damaged and countless numbers of indigenous animals destroyed. Thousands of firefighters and volunteers fought the fires, and it wasn't until February 2020 that the last fires were extinguished. Also, talk about more recent bushfires which are described in news reports on the web.

Figure 6.11 Wildfires in Australia

Ask children to imagine that they live in an area of Australia which is prone to wild-fires, and to describe the precautions they would take to keep themselves, their family, and their property safe. Working in groups, they start by choosing one of the following environments that best describes where they live:

1. Close to or among grass or paddocks
2. Close to or among dense or open bush
3. Near coastal shrub
4. Where suburbs meet the bush or grassland

Children draw a plan of their home/property, clearly showing the materials from which it is made and the environment in which it is located. Ask them to devise an explanation for why they have chosen to live there. Children search the web to find a photograph of an Australian home/property in an environment similar to the one they have chosen. They then assess the potential bushfire risks.

Consider the following when assessing the risks:

● The extent to which the home is surrounded by garden plants, including trees and bushes.
● The length and the size of the area of grass close to the home.
● Are trees close to or overhanging buildings?
● Whether branches are pruned.

Figure 6.12 Burnt home and property

- Is the home built from bushfire-safe building materials? (Metal or clay tile roof, brick, or concrete walls)
- Is there a site for water tanks/pumps?

Children discuss the bushfire risks and decide what they can do to reduce them. Groups display their plans and present their ideas. Ask children what they would expect to do if there was a bushfire sweeping towards their home. What action would they take? How would they prepare in advance?

Use the following scenario for a role-play activity in which children act out how they would prepare to stay and protect their property against a bushfire:

> A fire started close to our property on a day with a very high fire danger rating. It has been a long, hot, dry summer. The road to leave became blocked so we had to stay – luckily, we have a well-prepared property and can actively defend our house and keep my family safe. This role play presents what we have done to prepare and how we will respond to the fire.

These bushfire activities were adapted from resources published by the Geography Teacher's Association of Victoria.

Devastation in the developing world

Start by showing the children images and video clips of the devastation that can be caused by flash flooding in areas of the developing world. Lots of examples are on the

Figure 6.13 Image of flooding in Sub-Saharan Africa
Source: Mohamed Osman/Save the Children

web. Working in groups, children explore the FloodList website to discover the extent of flooding going on around the world. Children select and print a range of headlines which exemplify the global problem and pin them to a large world map. Identify the parts of the developing world which are most at risk from the climate crisis, and ask children to speculate about the problems local communities are likely to face if the crisis continues to get worse. Talk about how flooding and other natural disasters destroy harvests and homes, creating devastation from which people living in poverty find it hard to recover.

Research! Sub-Saharan Symposium

According to the World Bank, half of the world's poorest people live in Sub-Saharan Africa. As the name implies, these countries are mainly situated south of the Sahara Desert and are home to many of the most disadvantaged people in the world. In addition to high levels of extreme poverty, many people suffer from years of armed conflict, famine, disease, and frequent flooding, and climate change is making things worse.

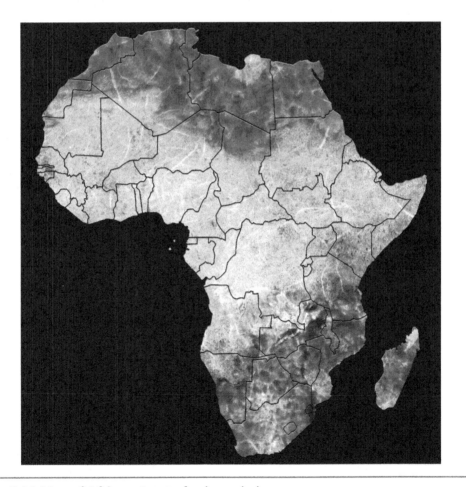

Figure 6.14 Map of Africa cut out of coloured glass

Children start by exploring the geography of different parts of Sub-Saharan Africa, including the name itself, which can be controversial. They use information sources to find out about:

- physical landscape, climate, vegetation, and wildlife;
- education systems, culture, disease, health care systems, economic issues, politics, and conflicts;
- life in urban and rural communities;
- technological, industrial, and agricultural development, including overseas aid;
- human impact on the environment;
- impact of climate change on communities.

Groups work on different points, frequently coming back together as a class to discuss their findings. Children agree on an executive summary to be published on the school's website or preferred social media platform. The summary should focus on the impact of climate change and the nature of the crisis faced by people who live in Sub-Saharan Africa.

Design! Beat the flood

If communities in Sub-Saharan Africa were more prepared for extreme weather, then they might be able to reduce the damage to their homes and repair them more quickly. Working in groups, children set about designing a home to withstand the effects of extreme weather, especially flooding. They need to think about the affordable materials that are likely to be available and where they will be sourced. Children debate the dilemmas faced by poor communities with regard to sourcing building materials.

Groups justify their designs with regard to the physical, social, and economic environment in which the family lives. From their designs, children build and test models of the home. Testing involves standing the model in water to show its flood-proof capabilities, then blasting it with water to show how it can stand up to storms. Publish videos of the project on the school's website or preferred social media platform.

Practical Action is a charity which is helping people in developing countries to adapt to climate change. For more ideas about ways to beat the climate crisis in the developing world, explore the education resources on the Practical Action website.

Human-elephant conflict

In this part, children explore ways of resolving conflict between wildlife and people that occurs as a consequence of communities living in areas where wildlife roams freely.

Amboseli National Park is a major wildlife safari park and a well-known tourist attraction in Kenya, which is famous for its elephants. As well as the elephants, many other types of animals live in the park, including giraffes, hippos, buffalo, zebra, wildebeest, lions, leopards, cheetahs, and hyenas.

A community living near Amboseli National Park in Southern Kenya has been experiencing more and more elephants coming into farmland areas and eating precious crops. Elephants have been coming into school grounds and damaging water storage facilities and school buildings. Elephants can also pose a danger to people in the community as they can occasionally cause injury and even loss of life. This is disastrous for the community. Many people already live in poverty and rely on farmland crops for food and as a vital income. Water is also a scarce and valuable resource. The community wants to find **sustainable** conservation solutions to address this problem of human-elephant conflict.

Read out this case-study from the WWF *Land for Life* website. Talk together about the issues the case-study highlights. Encourage children to speculate about why the elephants are damaging farmland, eating crops, and wandering into villages.

Talking points: True, false, or not sure?

- Elephants wander onto farmland because it used to be part of their natural habitat.
- Elephants eat farm crops because they are more nutritious than their normal food.
- Elephants eat farm crops because they cannot find enough food in the wild.
- Elephants wander into villages because they have nowhere else to go.
- Elephants wander into villages in search of food.
- Elephants wander into villages because they are lost.
- Elephants damage water storage facilities because they are desperate for water.
- Elephants look for water on farmland because their natural watering holes are dried up.
- Elephants wander into villages to find somewhere to hide from predators.
- Elephants wander into villages to attack the people who live there.
- Elephants wander into farmland areas because people have destroyed their natural habitats.

Groups discuss the talking points and try to agree on reasons why the community is experiencing problems with elephants. Do they think the climate crisis is likely to make the problem worse in the future? Ask children to justify their ideas.

Groups talk about what people might do to solve the problem of human-elephant conflict. Whose fault is it? Is it the elephants' fault for trespassing on the farmland, or it is the community's fault for destroying the elephants' natural habitat to create homes and clear land to grow crops? Or maybe it is nobody's fault! Perhaps, both the elephants and farmers have no choice in how they behave if they want to survive.

Conflict Resolution

Challenge children to design a solution to the human-elephant conflict that will suit both parties. That is, it will protect the elephants and also protect communities who live close to the elephants' habitat. Groups start by getting to know as much as they can about the elephants' habitat, as well as the type of farming carried by the people who live close to the National Park. They could also explore the Park's ecosystem and produce a food web. What part do elephants play in the ecosystem? Do they have any natural predators, or are humans their main source of danger? Find out about poaching in the National Park.

Apparently, elephants don't like bees or chili peppers, so children can think about how these can be used to safeguard crops. There are lots of other ideas on the web for children to consider. They should discuss the advantages and disadvantages of each one. Once groups have decided on their best solution, they need to think about how they will sell their idea to villagers in Kenya.

Conservation Consultation

Children imagine they are members of a conservation charity which is working with local people in Kenya to solve the elephant-human conflict problem, and have organised a meeting to present their ideas to local farmers. When planning the presentation, children should be aware that the farmers are unlikely to have much money, and will be reluctant to spend what little they have unless they think their idea will work and will also be cost-effective. Groups will need to persuade the farmers to put their solutions into action.

Presentations should be short and to the point:

- They should clarify the problem
- They should present and justify their solution
- They should identify the advantages and disadvantages of their solution
- They should explain why the farmers should choose their solution

The class acting as the farmers question each group and ask them to justify why theirs is the best solution. For example, they could ask:

- How long will the solution last? Elephants are very intelligent, and often learn new ways of getting what they want.
- How much will the solution cost? Can farmers afford it?
- Would the farmers require outside help to put the solution in place? Who would help them?
- Do children have any evidence that their solution has worked in other places?
- Does the solution bring with it additional benefits for the local community?
- Are the solutions sustainable? Does the solution meet the present needs, as well as the needs of both the farmers and the elephants in the future?

Create a large display which depicts the conflict between people and wildlife around the world. Use the outcomes of the case-study as the centre piece of the display. Children use recycled fabrics to make soft-toy elephants, polar bears, and other animals which are in conflict with humans and struggling to survive due to loss of habitat and global warming. Children can sell their toys to raise money to support the work of the World Wildlife Fund (WWF). The next chapter focuses on the impact the climate crisis is having on wildlife.

Information sources

Websites

- AWF Human Wildlife Conflict paper.pmd
- Bushfires – Lessons for the Primary Classroom – GTAV – Geography Teachers' Association of Victoria Inc.
- Bushfires in Australia – statistics & facts | Statista
- Flash flooding around the world – Bing video
- Greece wildfires: Evia island residents forced to evacuate – BBC News
- How to Protect Your Home and Garden from Elephants: 9 Steps (wikihow.com)
- Kenyan Wildlife Service (kws.go.ke)
- Land_For_Life_Teacher_Guide.pdf (wwf.org.uk)
- Wildlife – Amboseli National Parks
- 8 Ways to Keep Out an Elephant (stoppoaching-now.org)
- 'People are dying': how the climate crisis has sparked an exodus to the US | Global development | The Guardian
- Poverty Overview (worldbank.org)
- Swept Away: The Danger of Flooding in Developing Nations (childfund.org)

CHAPTER 7

IMPACT OF CLIMATE CRISIS ON WILDLIFE

Big idea: *Climate change is accelerating faster than expected and is threatening natural ecosystems and the fate of humanity.*

This chapter further develops children's understanding of the climate crisis by exploring its impact on wildlife. Part 1 provides subject knowledge for teachers regarding the impact the crisis is having on wildlife in three contrasting habitats: marine, polar, and tropical rainforests. The ideas presented provide real-life contexts to extend and enrich the primary curriculum.

The subject knowledge topics include:

- Alarming loss of plants
- Habitat destruction
- Deforestation fronts
- Tropical rainforests
- Polar regions
- Marine habitats

Part 1: Subject knowledge

Alarming loss of plants

Plants underpin life on Earth, yet we are destroying them at an alarming rate. Two in five of the world's plant species are at risk of extinction as a result of climate change, logging, and land-use change. Every year, scientists discover new species of plants that have not been scientifically described. In 2019, botanists recorded 1,942 new species of plants, many of which are disappearing before their roles in ecosystems and potential uses can be fully

DOI: 10.4324/9781003166276-7

explored. There are still vast numbers of species on this planet that we know nothing about, which potentially could provide valuable resources such as food, medicines, fibres, and biofuels. For example, recent discoveries in Brazil yielded two wild relatives of cassava that were previously unknown to science, as well as wild relatives of yams and sweet potatoes. The new species have the potential to be really important for future-proofing the cassava crop, which is a staple food for some 800 million people worldwide.

> Every time we lose a species, we lose an opportunity for humankind. . . . We are losing a race against time as we are probably losing species faster than we can find and name them.
>
> Professor Alexandre Antonelli, 2020

Professor Alexandre Antonelli is the Director of Science at the Royal Botanical Gardens, Kew, in the UK. He is also the lead author of the report *State of the World's Plants and Fungi 2020*, which focuses on the sustainable uses of plants and fungi for the benefit of humankind. It is the job of the Identification and Naming department at Kew to identify and name newly discovered plants and fungi, and then to find out their potential uses, and which are a priority for conservation.

Habitat destruction

Wildlife across the planet faces new challenges for survival because of the climate crisis. More frequent and intense drought, storms, heatwaves, rising sea levels, melting glaciers, and warming oceans can directly harm wildlife and destroy habitats.

> Climate change has reduced most animals' habitats by 18 percent, and that figure could shoot up to a quarter by the end of the century, researchers have warned. . . . Dr Robert Beyer in the University of Cambridge's Department of Zoology . . . said: "The habitat size of almost all known birds, mammals and amphibians is shrinking, primarily because of land conversion by humans as we continue to expand our agricultural and urban areas." . . . The loss of geographical range will force humans and animals to live closer together, increasing the likelihood of zoonotic diseases – ailments which originate in animals, such as coronavirus.
>
> (Express Newspaper, Nov 2020)

In recent years, it has been the wildlife in equatorial (tropical) regions that has suffered the most from climate change and human activity. Biodiversity in tropical rainforests is the richest on Earth, and people are destroying it by cutting down and removing trees on an industrial scale.

Deforestation fronts

Forests are the 'lungs of the Earth', and they play a critical role in the mitigation of climate change. They help provide the oxygen we all breathe and absorb huge amounts of carbon dioxide from the air.

Figure 7.1 Deforestation in Borneo

In the last century, more than half the world's tropical forests were destroyed, and continue to be destroyed today at an alarming rate. Despite protests from climate change activists, areas of forests greater than the size of South Africa have been cleared in the last thirty years. Already, half of the world's rainforest has been destroyed, and if today's rate of destruction continues, there will be no rainforests left by the end of the century.

The World Wildlife Fund (WWF) believes that in the next ten years, the bulk of global deforestation is likely to happen in 11 regions around the world. They have called these regions the 'deforestation fronts'. The fronts include forests in South America, Borneo and Sumatra, Southern Africa, the Greater Mekong region, New Guinea, and Eastern Australia. For each of these regions, the WWF provides reasons why people are clearing the land. These reasons include logging, agriculture, livestock farming, mining, infrastructure projects, charcoal and fuelwood, and large dams for hydroelectricity. The forests are also being damaged by wildfires due to prolonged high temperatures, some of which may or may not have been started deliberately.

The deforestation fronts include the world's remaining tropical forests, home to a rich diversity of wildlife, including endangered animals such as elephants, jaguars, tigers, and orang-utans, whose name means 'man of the forest'. Rainforests are the undisputed champions of biodiversity among the world's ecosystems, containing more than 50% of the plant and animal species on Earth. Therefore, the future of all these species depends on the future of the forests in the deforestation fronts.

Tropical rainforests

Tropical rainforests cover about 7% of the Earth's surface. The forests experience rainfall throughout the year, with short intermittent dry spells. The climate is hot and humid, with temperatures ranging from 20°C to 34°C. The forests are mainly made up of tall, straight trees with few branches below the canopy. The bark on the trees is generally thin and smooth, often making one type of tree difficult to distinguish from another. Seventy percent of the plants in a rainforest are trees. Many types of animals can be found in a tropical rainforest forest, with the canopy being the most populated habitat. Birds and monkeys are the most common mammals in the canopy, while the dark forest floor supports reptiles and large mammals, and is teeming with insects. Although all tropical rainforests support similar types of animals and plants, they each have their own particular species.

The Amazon Rainforest is the largest tropical rainforest, covering a vast area spanning eight South American countries, and contains half of the Earth's remaining tropical forests. One in ten of all the known species on Earth live in the Amazon. As the forests are cut down and burned to make way for farming, wildlife habitats literally go up in smoke. Animals in danger due to habitat loss include jaguars, harpy eagles, pink

Figure 7.2 Goeldi's marmoset

dolphins, and thousands of birds and butterflies. Tree dwellers are amongst the animals in most danger; these include the amazing two-toed sloths, pygmy marmosets, saddle-back and emperor tamarins, and the fabulous Goeldi's marmoset.

Habitat destruction in the Congo Rainforests

Habitat destruction can be found in most rainforests around the world. In the Congo Rainforests in Central Africa, deforestation is not as widespread as in the Amazon. However, areas of forest are being cleared for large-scale agriculture at an increasing rate. Logging roads are being built to provide easier access to the interior; in some areas, these are being used by poachers to hunt elephants. There has been more than a 60% decline in the forest elephant population in the last ten years.

People who live in the Congo Basin slash and burn the forest to make room to grow crops, destroying and splitting wildlife habitats as they do so. As their habitats are fragmented and reduced, it is easier for hunters to find and kill the animals. Animals at risk include chimpanzees, bonobos, antelope, and gorillas, which are being killed in large numbers for 'bush meat' by hunters who are themselves struggling to survive. Bonobos and chimpanzees look very similar, which is not surprising since they are closely related. Perhaps what is surprising is how closely related we are to bonobos and chimpanzees, both of which share 98.7% of their DNA with humans. This makes them our closest living relatives amongst all the species of animals which inhabit the Earth. So, why are we not doing more to protect our own 'cousins'?!

Figure 7.3 Baby Gorilla

Polar regions

Wildlife in the polar regions is also under threat due to habitat loss. In this case, wildlife habitats are being destroyed by rising sea and air temperatures. Polar bears are the Arctic's top predator, as well as the largest bear on Earth. They are marine mammals that rely on the ocean to survive, and are uniquely adapted to living on the Arctic ice. For example, polar bears have a thick layer of body fat and a waterproof coat which protects them against the cold wind and freezing sea ice. They also have thick, transparent fur to keep warm. Their transparent fur appears white in bright sunlight, similar in colour to ice and snow, providing them with camouflage when hunting. Polar bears are excellent swimmers with large paws and short claws that enable them to walk on ice. They also have powerful vision for seeing in the dark and the water, and a highly specialised, high-fat and energy-efficient diet.

Polar bears need to travel across the sea ice to hunt for seals, which are their main source of food. Due to the climate crisis, the sea ice is melting and breaking up, making hunting far more difficult. Consequently, polar bears are increasingly spending more time on land and are frequently attracted to areas where people live, which can result in them being killed. Polar bears are listed as a threatened species. This means, if things don't improve in the near future, they are likely to be in danger of extinction. Other Arctic animals whose habitats are affected by climate change include walruses, reindeer, seals, narwhals, arctic foxes, orcas, lemmings, beluga whales, musk oxen, and red knot birds.

Figure 7.4 Polar bears feeding

The ocean surrounding the Antarctic continent provides habitats for a large range of wildlife, including 15 species of whale and dolphin and five species of penguin. The ocean's ecosystem is sustained by a multitude of tiny plankton, which thrive in the nutrient-rich waters. Krill and small fish feed on the plankton, which in turn become prey for larger animals such as whales, seals, and penguins. The emperor penguin is the world's biggest penguin, and perhaps the most well-known and loved. It is only found in the Antarctic, and its existence is threatened by the climate crisis.

> Antarctica still blows my mind. It is vast, remote, otherworldly and beautiful beyond imagination. But it is also fragile and vulnerable to the worst effects of climate change and fishing. I've spent more than two years living on the ice and two decades working to ensure that the Antarctic remains protected for future generations.
>
> Ron Downie, Polar Programme Manager for WWF

Like polar bears in the Arctic, emperor penguins are especially vulnerable to climate change because they rear their young on sea ice. The Antarctic sea ice has been melting at a rapid rate in recent years, creating an uncertain future for the penguins. In some places, numbers of emperor penguins have declined by up to 50%, with one colony off the Antarctic Peninsula completely wiped out.

In some areas, scientists have found krill numbers to be declining. Krill are a very important source of food, and their decline threatens not only the penguins, but also whales, seals, and other consumers in the Antarctic food web. Research shows that krill numbers have dropped by about 80% in the last 40 years due to the loss of sea ice during winter. The decline in krill may also help explain declines seen in several species of penguins, including the emperor.

Figure 7.5 Penguin adrift on melting ice

Marine habitats

The marine biome covers about 71% of the Earth's surface and includes oceans, coral reefs, and estuaries. Marine algae are the main primary producers in this biome. Like plants, they use chlorophyll for photosynthesis, but unlike plants, they do not have roots, stems, or leaves, and do not produce seeds or flowers. Marine algae supply much of the world's oxygen and absorb immense amounts of carbon dioxide from the air. There are many types of algae, which come in all shapes and sizes. They range from tiny organisms that form part of the plankton floating in the ocean, to giant seaweed which floats on the ocean's surface. Phytoplankton are a microscopic type of marine algae. The word plankton comes from the Greek word *planktos*, which means "drifter", so phytoplankton can be interpreted as 'drifting plants', although they are not officially classified as part of the plant kingdom. Another type of plankton that drifts about in the oceans is called zooplankton (wandering or drifting animals). Zooplankton is a consumer and feeds on phytoplankton. In turn, zooplankton provide food for fish, crustaceans, and other animals, including whales.

The climate crisis is causing drastic changes in marine ecosystems, including the seas surrounding the UK. At the bottom of the food chain, rising water temperatures are causing a decline in plankton, which is, in turn, causing a decline in sand eels which feed on them. This has a knock-on effect further up the chain, with the animals who feed on the eels struggling to find enough food. Sand eels are a staple food for puffins, which are particularly vulnerable. With less food available to them, puffins are not breeding well and their numbers are declining. Other seabirds, such as kittiwake and guillemots, that feed on sand eels are also in decline.

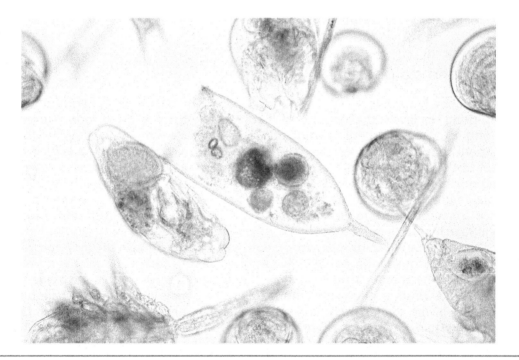

Figure 7.6 Marine plankton under the microscope

Global warming hits sea creatures hardest

> Global warming has caused twice as many ocean-dwelling species as land-dwelling species to disappear from their habitats, a unique Rutgers-led study found. The greater vulnerability of sea creatures may significantly impact human communities that rely on fish and shellfish for food and economic activity, according to the study published in the journal Nature.
>
> Phys.org, April, 2019

This study was first to compare the sensitivity of cold-blooded marine and land animals to global warming. They found that marine animals were twice as likely to be forced out of their habitats, compared to land animals. The reasons given were that land animals could more easily find shelter in forests, shaded areas, and underground. The only way sea animals can adapt is by moving to cooler water. This means that continued global warming is likely to trigger the loss of marine animals from established habitats, and as a result do great damage to marine ecosystems.

Around the world, there are reports of marine animals moving to cooler waters to escape the rising temperatures. In the USA, scientists have found that American lobster, black sea bass, red hake, and over a hundred other populations of marine creatures have already shifted north to cooler waters. Studies in Britain show that cod and haddock in the North Sea are moving further north into deeper water in response to rising sea temperatures. At the same time, greater numbers of squid, red mullet, sardines, and sea bass are moving up from the south as their waters continue to warm. The migration of marine life is seen by many scientists as a sign that the climate crisis is beginning to have a serious impacts on the Earth's oceans.

Whales and dolphins

Climate change is a major threat to whales and dolphins. Warming and acidification of oceans, rising sea levels, the loss of polar habitats, and the decline of food sources are some of the key reasons these amazing marine mammals are threatened by the climate crisis. Scientists are concerned that whales and dolphins may not be able to adapt quickly enough to the environmental changes to be able to survive. As the oceans warm up, moving north may be the only option for some species. However, depending on their habitats, migration may not be possible for some. For example, the northern Indian Ocean is fringed by land, reducing the ability of whales and dolphins to move further north in search of cooler waters.

Whales play a part in controlling the amount of carbon dioxide in the air by providing nutrients for phytoplankton. Whales dive to great depths to feed and come up to the surface to breathe and defecate. In doing so, their actions serve to circulate oxygen and their nutritious waste in the water: this is called the 'whale pump'. The 'whale pump' provides life-giving oxygen and nutrients for the phytoplankton and helps maintain a healthy ecosystem. Phytoplankton produce half of the Earth's oxygen and absorb huge amounts of carbon dioxide from the atmosphere, which is about equivalent to that absorbed by four rainforests.

Figure 7.7 Whale breaching the water

Great Barrier Reef

The coral reef system stretches for over 2,300 kilometres up Australia's northeast coast and includes 900 islands. The Great Barrier Reef is so large that it can be seen by astronauts on the International Space Station, and is the biggest single living structure in the world. Coral reefs are easy to spot from space because the iridescent blues of shallow lagoons contrast sharply with the dark blues of deep water, which they divide.

Corals are sea animals that remain in the same place. They are known as colonial organisms because they are composed of hundreds of thousands of tiny animals, called polyps. Each one of the polyps has a stomach and a mouth surrounded by tentacles. The polyp uses its tentacles to capture its food, clear away debris, and to defend itself. Depending on their size, polyps prey on a range of animals, from tiny zooplankton to small fish.

Scientists have found that marine heatwaves can destroy some corals through a process called bleaching. Corals are normally covered in colourful algae which nourish it. Corals are sensitive to temperature, and if the water becomes too warm, they shed the algae, turning them completely white. Without the algae they are more vulnerable and are likely to be destroyed by repeated bleaching events. Also, rising levels of acidity in the oceans is causing massive damage to coral reefs around the world. Ocean acidification is particularly damaging to animals that build their skeletons and shells from calcium carbonate. Acid erodes their shells and also inhibits their growth. Clams, mussels, crabs, coral, and types of plankton are some of the wildlife which can be badly affected.

Figure 7.8 The Great Barrier Reef

Part 2: Working towards the big idea

This part provides ideas and activities which enable children to work towards under-standing the big idea within a framework of good practice. Children's learning starts by exploring how deforestation is destroying valuable ecosystems which sequester carbon dioxide and help limit global warming. Activities provide opportunities to learn about some of the world's most endangered animal species. Focus then moves to the polar regions, where children work on their understanding of the problems faced by polar bears due to changes in their environment caused by global warming. In this part, chil-dren debate whether polar bears can survive by adapting to the new conditions. The bigger picture draws children's attention to the part marine algae play in sequestering carbon dioxide, as well as providing much of the Earth's oxygen. Focus is also placed on the impact the climate crisis is having on marine ecosystems. Learning directly related to the primary science curriculum includes living things in their habitats and properties and changes of materials.

Children have opportunities to develop and use the following science and design technology skills:

- Work collaboratively towards common goals.
- Use different types of scientific enquiries, including data gathering and fair testing.
- Research using secondary sources.

- Generate, develop, model, and communicate ideas through discussion, sketches, and prototypes.
- Communicate outcomes of their research, enquiry, and design in different ways.
- Apply their learning in real-life contexts.

Exploring children's ideas

Art! Lungs of the Earth

Start by showing children a picture of a tropical rainforest, and describe the forest as the 'lungs of the Earth'. Ask them whether they think 'lungs of the Earth' is a good analogy. Talk about how trees take in carbon dioxide through their leaves and 'breathe' out oxygen. Remind children that forests reduce greenhouse gases in the atmosphere by sequestering (capturing) huge amounts of carbon dioxide from the air. Talk about deforestation and how it is contributing to the climate crisis.

Challenge children to create a cartoon-style image of a tropical rainforest depicting it as the 'lungs of the Earth'. Children start by researching how cartoonists have already depicted issues related to the climate crisis.

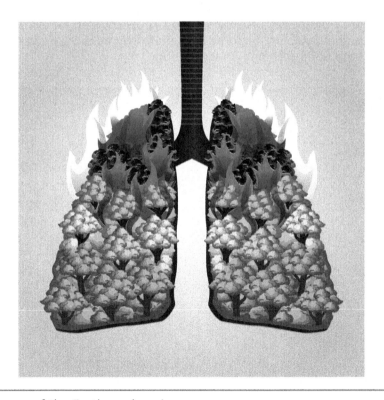

Figure 7.9 Lungs of the Earth are burning

Debate! Deforestation fronts

Talk about how tropical forests are being destroyed at an alarming rate, and if this continues, scientists predict that the tropical forests could be totally destroyed in the children's lifetime. Focus children's attention on the 'deforestation fronts' identified by the WWF. Point out that these are the regions where the bulk of deforestation is likely to happen in the next ten years.

Working in groups, children use information sources to explore the reasons why people are clearing rainforests in the regions identified as deforestation fronts. Groups come together to share their findings and debate whether the people really need to chop down the trees. What else could they do? If the children had the opportunity to talk to the people in these areas, what would they say to them to persuade them to stop clearing the forests? Children debate the options open to the land clearers, with one set of children representing those clearing the land, and another set acting on behalf of the conservationists. Should people in the developing world be given financial incentives to stop destroying the forests? What else can be done before it is too late?

Imagine! Undiscovered habitats

Children produce creative paintings of an imaginary, undiscovered part of a tropical rainforest. Their paintings depict the climate, plants, and the habitat of a previously unknown animal species. Children tell stories about their undiscovered rainforests from the point of view of the explorer/scientist who first discovered it. Talk together about how the plants and animals are adapted to the environment. Address any misconceptions related to their understanding of adaptation.

Figure 7.10 Bonobos in natural habitat

Story-telling! Our closest relatives

Our closest relatives in the animal kingdom are chimpanzees and bonobos, with whom we share about 99% of our DNA. In fact, chimps and bonobos are more closely related to humans than they are to other apes, such as gorillas. Although chimps, bonobos, and humans are closely related, they each have their own distinctive physical features and behaviour. Working in groups, children use information sources to compare these three 'cousins' both socially and physically. Children may be surprised to find that we have more in common with our 'African cousins' than they might imagine. Groups come together to compare human behaviour with that of chimpanzees and bonobos, and to tell stories about the way their 'cousins' survive and the dangers they face.

Campaign! Save critically endangered animals

An endangered species is a type of living thing that is threatened by extinction. 'Critically endangered' means that these animals are very close to extinction. Indonesia and Malaysia have a number of critically endangered mammal species, mainly due to the destruction of forest habitats to grow palm oil. These include the Sumatran orang-utan, Bornean orang-utan, Sumatran rhino, Sumatran elephant, Javan rhino, and the Sundra tiger.

Working in groups, children plan media campaigns to save some of the most critically endangered animals around the world. They start by exploring the species list of critically endangered animals on the WWF website and choose the animal species for which they would like to campaign.

Figure 7.11 Javan Rhino

To help plan a campaign, children explore the type of conservation work being done by wildlife charities. The WWF have some fascinating stories about animal conservation to share with children, such as the work they have done to save the Black Rhino by moving them to new areas with suitable habitats. Another conservation charity is the Jane Goodall Institute. Jane Goodall has dedicated her life to studying and protecting chimpanzees. Sadly, our African cousins are in danger of extinction and need our help to survive. Jane Goodall's life story is fascinating, and children can explore the work she has done as scientist, activist, and conservationist.

Once groups have explored the work being done by wildlife charities, they can start to sketch out and organise their own campaigns. Here are some things for children to think about when planning their campaign to save an endangered species:

1. *What is the main problem?*
   - Is the problem caused by climate change, loss of habitat, poaching, or something else?
   - Who or what is mainly responsible for the problem?

2. *What is the solution?*
   - Is the solution political? Can governments do more to help?
   - What are conservation trusts doing to help? Are they doing enough?
   - Can the introduction of new technology and/or agriculture help?
   - Given the opportunity, what would they (the children) do to solve the problem?

3. *What are the advantages and disadvantages to their solution?*
   - Are the endangered species the only winners as a result of their solution?
   - Will their solution disadvantage local communities?
   - Will their solution disadvantage other wildlife?

4. *How will they present and publish their campaign?*
   - Who will be the target of their campaign?
   - How will they present and communicate their ideas?
   - How will they bring the problems to the attention of the public?

Children could present their campaign to a special assembly of the school community. They could also publish leaflets to be distributed in the local community or publish an article in the school science magazine. They could get their message out in the form of a blog on the school's website or preferred social media platform, or write an article for a local or national newspaper. Campaigning also provides opportunities for children to collaborate with other schools using social conferencing platforms, such as Zoom.

Campaigning not only spreads the message that much of the world's wildlife is threatened; it also makes children's learning more meaningful. Not every child can be a Greta Thunberg, but they can all make a contribution to protecting the natural world. Small seeds of awareness which are sown today may grow and blossom in ways which change the world in the future.

Information sources

Websites

- African Elephants and Climate Change | Pages | WWF (worldwildlife.org)

- Bonobo | Species | WWF (worldwildlife.org)
- Bonobos Join Chimps as Closest Human Relatives | Science | AAAS
- Chimpanzees | Species | WWF (worldwildlife.org)
- Climate Change | African Wildlife Foundation (awf.org)
- Deforestation Fronts | WWF (panda.org)
- Deforestation and Forest Degradation | Threats | WWF (worldwildlife.org)
- Endangered – The Congo Rainforest (weebly.com)
- Endangered species threatened by unsustainable palm oil production | Stories | WWF (worldwildlife.org)
- Home – Jane Goodall Institute UK
- Illegal Wildlife Trade Classroom Resources | WWF
- IUCN Red List of Threatened Species
- Land for Life Schools Resources | WWF
- Our Planet Classroom Resources | WWF
- Rainforest Habitat facts and photos (nationalgeographic.com)
- Saving the Rhinos | Stories | WWF (worldwildlife.org)
- Species List | Endangered, Vulnerable, and Threatened Animals | WWF (worldwildlife.org)
- The endangered bonobo: Africa's forgotten ape (awf.org)
- The Congo Rainforest (mongabay.com)
- WWF is saving black rhinos by moving them | Stories | WWF (worldwildlife.org)
- 10 Ways Chimps and Humans are the same (janegoodall.ca)

Working on scientific understanding

This part provides opportunities for children to explore the impact climate change is having on wildlife habitats in the Arctic Region, and at the same time work on their scientific understanding of adaptation and states of matter, and develop their scientific enquiry skills.

Polar regions

Children will likely be familiar with some of the species of animals which live in the polar regions, although they may be less familiar with the geography and vegetation. Begin by using maps to identify and compare the Arctic and Antarctic regions. Identify areas of sea ice and land ice. Point out that unlike the Antarctic, there is no land at the North Pole. All of the ice cap surrounding the North Pole is floating on top of the Arctic Ocean.

Enquire! Melting sea ice

Use images and video clips from the web to show how ice in the polar regions is melting due to global warming. Children model the effects of global warming on sea ice in the classroom, using ice cubes, paper cups, thermometers, and a source of warm water.

Figure 7.12 Polar bear adrift on melting sea ice

Working in groups, children plan an investigation to discover the relationship between the water temperature and the rate at which ice floating in the water melts. Focus their attention on fair testing. They record their results by plotting graphs of temperature of the water against time for the ice to melt. Is there a direct relationship between water temperatures and melt time? Talk about how small rises in temperature could lead to significant amounts of sea ice melting over long periods of time.

Use this opportunity to talk about states of matter. Compare the particle structure of ice and water, and model how heating the solid water (ice) makes the particles vibrate vigorously, resulting in the collapse of the solid structure into that of a liquid (water). For more information refer to Loxley et al. (2018).

The UK Arctic Research Station

Introduce children to the UK Arctic Research Station, which was established in the research village of Ny-Ålesund (Svalbard), in 1991. It provides facilities and accommodation for researchers from UK universities and research institutes who want to carry out environmental research, much of which is to do with climate change.

Children visit the Svalbard Science website to discover what the scientists are doing. They can use the webcams to look around the research village, where Arctic scientists from around the world are based. Talk together about the types of people who become Arctic researchers. What characteristics do they need to possess?

Polar bear problems

Read out the following extract from the Health and Safety Guidelines provided to scientists by the UK Arctic Research Station:

Figure 7.13 Polar bear wandering downtown

For protection from attack by polar bear each group must carry a NERC owned or approved rifle outside the immediate station area. **Please note, personnel will not be allowed to work alone in the field** . At the station manager's discretion, rifles are allocated to those who have attended a Kings Bay rifle training course in Ny-Ålesund. Any queries on the above, please contact the Station Manager.

Encourage children to speculate about the need for scientists in the Arctic to carry a rifle when outside the research village. Why would a polar bear want to attack them? What do polar bears normally eat? Isn't it risky for the bears to come close to the village? Why would they take the chance? What are they looking for?

Introduce polar bears as the Arctic's top predator and talk about how they are uniquely adapted to living on the arctic ice. Use images and video clips from the web to illustrate how they travel across the sea ice to hunt for seals, which are their main source of food. Point out that melting sea ice is making hunting far more difficult for the polar bears. Consequently, polar bears are increasingly spending more time on land and are frequently attracted to areas where people live, which can result in them being killed.

Can polar bears adapt to life on land?

Talk about how polar bears are listed as a threatened species. This means, if sea ice continues to melt, they are likely to be in danger of extinction. Ask children what the bears could do once the sea ice has melted. Could they adapt to life on land?

Talking points: True, false, or not sure?

- Once the ice has melted, polar bears could live in the sea.
- Polar bears could quickly adapt to life on land.
- They could live in forests with other types of bears.
- They would be well-suited to living in mountain regions.
- They could live on small islands where there are lots of birds and small mammals to eat.
- They could catch seals that live on the shore.
- They could learn to catch fish in rivers and streams.
- They could learn to eat vegetation, including fruit and berries.
- They could learn to eat insects, worms, and other invertebrates.

Working in groups, children respond to the talking points. Listen to their ideas and address misconceptions. Point out that polar bears are marine mammals that rely on the ice and the ocean to survive. Ask children to list as many things as they can which make polar bears suited to their Arctic environment. Relevant information can be found in Part 1. Debate whether polar bears can adapt to another environment if global warming continues. Encourage children to speculate about different possibilities. If climate change continues and the ice continues to melt, what do the children predict will happen to the polar bears?

Enquire! Arctic research

Working in groups, children imagine they are environmental scientists who want to carry out research in the Arctic. The UK Arctic Research Station is open to all kinds of research. Scientists who would like to use the station must submit plans for their research to the Natural Environment Research Council (NERC). The plans are then assessed and, if approved, they will receive a letter inviting them to use the centre.

In their application, they need to state the objectives of their research and the nature of the field work, including the details of the experiments they intend to carry out. The centre is only open between March and September, and the numbers of scientists who can be accommodated is limited. Therefore, they will be competing against other scientists for a place at the station, so they need to clearly explain why their research is important and why they should be offered a place.

Safety is very important, especially in the Arctic, where conditions can be challenging. So, when planning for the trip, children need to decide on the clothing and equipment to take with them. They also need to agree a set of health and safety rules to follow when doing work in the field. Children compare the clothing they choose and their health and safety rules with the advice provided on the Svalbard Science website.

Groups should present their applications to the class, who act as the NERC committee. Members of the committee question the groups about the nature of their research and how they will carry it out. What tests will they make? How will they make their tests fair? What data will they collect? How will they record their results? What do they expect to find out? Encourage children to listen to each other's ideas. Interactions should be supportive and respectful. Identify and address misconceptions.

Figure 7.14 Dressed for the cold

Safeguarding seeds for the future

Plants underpin life on Earth, yet we are destroying them at an alarming rate. Two in five of the world's plant species are at risk of extinction as a result of climate change, logging, and land-use change. Use information from Part 1 to talk about how plants are being destroyed before they have even been identified.

Describe how seed banks provide a way of safeguarding plants for the future, especially those which are in danger of extinction. Talk about Svalbard as the home of the Global Seed Vault, which stores duplicate seeds from other seed vaults around the world. Its purpose is to provide back-up to individual collections in the event that the original seeds are lost due to natural disasters, human conflict, mismanagement, or any other circumstances. Talk about why the Svalbard Global Seed Vault is commonly referred to as the Doomsday Vault.

Research! Why choose Svalbard?

Working in groups, children use information sources to explore why Svalbard was chosen to be the site of the Global Seed Vault. Why would the seeds be safer in Svalbard than in other parts of the world if there was a major world crisis? Groups come together to share and debate their ideas.

Enquire! Storing seeds

Are seeds best stored in cold or warm conditions? Do they need to be kept moist or do they store better when they are dry? Are they better kept in the dark or in the light? Can seeds be stored in ice? Groups plan investigations to find out the best way to store seeds. Talk about controlling variables to ensure the tests are fair. Children can collect and store a variety of seeds in autumn, and plant them in spring to see which germinate the quickest. Grow them on into the summer to see which grow best. Groups collect data on each plant and draw conclusions about the best way to store seeds. Children design packets for their seeds using photographs of the fully grown plant, including instructions for how to store and grow them. Link this enquiry to curriculum work on plants.

Information sources

Websites

- Arctic science – Discovering the Arctic
- As Sea Ice Shrinks, Can Polar Bears Survive on Land? (nationalgeographic.com)
- Climate Change (arcticcentre.org)
- Films – Arctic Office
- How Is The Polar Bear Adapted To Its Environment? – WorldAtlas
- Hungry Polar Bear Ambushes Seal | The Hunt | BBC Earth – Bing video
- North Pole | National Geographic Society
- Polar bear kills man camping on remote Norwegian island | The Independent | The Independent
- Polar Regions | Habitats | WWF (worldwildlife.org)
- Polar Bear | Species | WWF (worldwildlife.org)
- Svalbard science – Discovering the Arctic
- The Arctic Research Programme – Discovering the Arctic
- 11 Arctic species affected by climate change | WWF
- Why are glaciers and sea ice melting? | Pages | WWF (worldwildlife.org)

The bigger picture

In this part, children discover that when looking at the bigger picture, it is the smallest things which have the most to contribute to the health of the planet.

Talk! Marine algae

It is often the large creatures towards the top of the food chain, such as polar bears, sharks, whales, and dolphins, that first come to mind when thinking about marine habitats. However, it is worth reminding children that these creatures could not survive without the producers, such as marine algae. Introduce children to marine algae as the heroes of marine ecosystems. They not only provide food for a wide variety of marine creatures, but they also supply much of the world's oxygen and absorb immense amounts of carbon dioxide from the air. Three cheers for marine algae!

Talk about how marine algae form part of the plankton floating in the ocean, and describe how they produce and store food in the same way as plants. Working in groups, children use information sources to explore different types of marine algae and the ecosystems which they support. Children create food webs to illustrate interdependency and balance in the ecosystems. Talk about how rising sea temperatures are causing a decline in phytoplankton, which in turn causes a decline in animals further up the food chain.

Art: Marine ecosystem

Based on images of different types of plankton, children can have fun creating their own unique cartoon images of plankton, similar to the clip art found on the web. In a similar cartoon style, they create picture books, suitable for younger children, which character-ise a marine ecosystem. They can make up names for the main protagonists such as Polly Plankton, Sally Shark, Peter Puffin, or Wally Whale.

Figure 7.15 Cartoon image of microscopic plankton

Research! Mapping endangered species

Children use information sources to identify and explore the habitats of endangered marine animal species. Their findings can be plotted on a huge map of the world and displayed prominently in the classroom. This can be an ongoing project, with endangered species being added to the map throughout the term. Children create a fact file for each of the endangered species on the map, which contains:

1. The name of the animal species
2. A description of its habitat, including the climate
3. Characteristics which make it suitable to its habitat
4. Its food sources
5. Its predators
6. Reasons for why it is endangered
7. A review of what is being done to protect the species
8. A prediction about whether the species are likely to survive in the future

Children analyse their data to discover whether animal species that live in particular types of habitats are more likely to be in danger of extinction. Encourage them to draw conclusions about the main dangers to marine wildlife: is it climate change, pollution, over-fishing, or something else?

Enquire! The effects of ocean acidification

Talk about how the oceans are becoming more acidic due to the absorption of carbon dioxide. Point out that acidification is particularly damaging to animals that build their skeletons from calcium carbonate, because the acid erodes their shells. Encourage children to list animals they think will be affected, such as clams, mussels, crabs, corals, and types of plankton.

Children model the impact of acidification on animals with shells by using carbonated drinks and pieces of chalk (calcium carbonate). Carbonated drinks have carbon dioxide gas added to provide their fizzy taste. The carbon dioxide dissolves in the water to form carbonic acid, just as it does in the oceans, thus making the drink acidic.

Working in groups, children test the pH levels of various carbonated drinks, including soda water, colas, diet colas, and fizzy fruit drinks. They then compare their effects on chalk over periods of time. Is the most acidic liquid also the most corrosive? Does temperature influence the rate at which the chalk reacts with an acidic liquid? Children record their results and draw conclusions. What does their enquiry tell them about the problems caused by the climate crisis?

Groups present the results of their enquiries in the form of a scientific paper to be given at a scientific conference in the classroom. The presentation should start with a justification of their methods, then a summary of their findings and conclusions. Finally, they explain the significance of their findings with regard to possible future problems for marine wildlife.

Research! Crisis time for the world's largest natural wonder

Introduce children to the Great Barrier Reef in Australia, the biggest single living structure in the world. Talk about how the reef is made from coral, which is the external skeleton of hundreds of thousands of tiny animals.

Working in groups, children use information sources to explore the ecosystem of the reef, including the symbiotic relationship between the coral and the marine algae. Groups come together to share their findings and discuss the impact the climate crisis is having on the coral. Talk together about the cause of the bleaching. Without the algae to help sustain them, corals struggle to survive. Children make predictions about the future of the coral ecosystem if the coral continues to be destroyed. Children write a creative, scientifically accurate account of the plight of the Great Barrier Reef in the form of an illustrated article for a non-scientific magazine. The article could be entitled: *Crisis time for the world's largest natural wonder.* Before writing the article, children should explore the writing styles in some appropriate magazines.

Figure 7.16 Coral bleaching

Information resources

Websites

- Blue Planet – Live Lesson – BBC Teach
- Coral reefs and climate change: from cradle to an early grave | WWF
- Global warming hits sea creatures hardest (phys.org)
- How climate change relates to oceans | Stories | WWF (worldwildlife.org)
- Marine Ecosystems | National Geographic Society
- Marine Food Chain (nationalgeographic.com)
- Plankton | National Geographic Society
- The marine biome (berkeley.edu)
- The Marine Biome: Facts, Pictures, Ecosystems, Species & Threats (activewild.com)
- The Ocean Is Getting More Acidic – What That Actually Means (nationalgeographic. com)
- What are phytoplankton? (noaa.gov)
- What are Phytoplankton? (nasa.gov)
- What are plankton? (noaa.gov)
- WWF TES Classroom Resource – Oceans and Plastics Pollution | WWF
- Zooplankton Facts (softschools.com)

CHAPTER 8
THE WORLD WE MUST CREATE

Big Idea: *We need to change the way we live in order to reduce carbon emissions to net zero, and prevent irreparable damage to our planet.*

This chapter provides opportunities for children to develop their understanding of some of the actions we need to take to address the climate crisis. Part 1 sets out the ideas behind the actions, with a focus on reducing carbon emissions to net zero by 2050 and limiting warming to 1.5°C above pre-industrial levels. The 'world we must create' provides an important and compelling real-life context in which to teach relevant parts of the primary curriculum.

Topics include:

- Change our diet
- Plant more trees
- Green-up outdoor spaces
- Stop burning fossil fuels
- Improve home insulation
- Develop low-carbon energy
- Use low-carbon transport
- Develop carbon capture technologies
- Offset carbon emissions
- Choose our future

Part 1: Subject knowledge

The evidence is clear: we are responsible for the climate crisis and if we don't do something about it soon, it will be too late:

> "We are the last generation that can prevent irreparable damage to our planet," General Assembly President María Fernanda Espinosa Garcés

Figure 8.1 Global warming target

(Ecuador) warned the gathering in her opening remarks, stressing that 11 years are all that remain to avert catastrophe. Highlighting the meeting's theme, Ms. Espinosa called for an intergenerational approach to climate change. . . . Drawing inspiration from the thousands of students worldwide demanding tangible action, she called on world leaders to make 2020 the last year carbon emissions increase due to human activities.

United Nations, March 2019

As I write this chapter, world leaders are preparing for the 2021 COP 26 meeting in Glasgow amid calls for ever more ambitious targets for reducing greenhouse gases. However, as the politicians continue to talk, global carbon emissions continue to rise. Many people around the world are increasingly frustrated by the lack of tangible action, especially young activists, such as Greta Thunberg, who are worried that too little is being done to prevent the climate crisis becoming a global disaster. The purpose of this chapter is to raise children's awareness of some of the actions we need to take to limit warming to 1.5 degrees Celsius, by reducing carbon emissions to net zero by 2050.

Change our diet

The Intergovernmental Panel on Climate Change (IPCC) has called for a radical transformation of the food system. The panel found that up to 37% of the world's total greenhouse gases come from the production of food and its refrigeration and transportation, and that about a third of the food is lost or wasted. Methane emitted from farm animals, especially cows, was found to be one of the major contributors to climate change.

We can play a part in combating the climate crisis by adopting a balanced diet to improve our health and the health of the planet. The IPCC recommends that people eat a lot less meat, especially pork and beef, and eat more plant-based foods.

Debra Roberts, Co-Chair of IPCC Working Group II, wrote:

> Balanced diets featuring plant-based foods, such as coarse grains, legumes, fruits and vegetables, and animal-sourced food produced sustainably in low greenhouse gas emission systems, present major opportunities for . . . limiting climate change.

The changes to our diets mean that many people will be asked to reduce their meat consumption by 77% and their consumption of dairy products by 40%. Clearly, saving the planet is not just about planting more trees and using fewer fossil fuels; it requires cultural changes that many people may be very reluctant to adopt.

Plant more trees

Trees are nature's way of controlling the amounts of carbon dioxide in the air. Trees remove carbon dioxide from the air through their leaves and store it in the wood of their trunks, roots, and branches through a process called photosynthesis. To picture photosynthesis, think of leaves as food-making machines (organs). They start by collecting the ingredients, which are carbon dioxide from the air, and water and nutrients from the soil. They then use energy from the Sun to 'cook up' the ingredients to make a sugary food, which is stored in different parts of the plant. The trees use some of this food to grow, and store the rest in their leaves, fruits, branches, trunk, and roots.

Because they grow so big, trees need a lot of carbon dioxide, and therefore capture huge amounts of carbon dioxide over their long lives. In some cases, carbon can be locked away in trees for hundreds of years. Most of the carbon sequestered by a tree is locked away inside its wood. Carbon in the leaves of deciduous trees is not stored for long, because it is recycled back into the air when the leaves decompose. Oak trees are especially good for carbon capture because they have large canopies and are made of dense, heavy wood. Horse chestnuts and evergreens, such as conifers and pines, are also good carbon sequesters. Beside trees, long-lived woody plants (shrubs) can be useful carbon sequesters.

In addressing the climate crisis, few actions are more urgent, or as simple, as planting trees. In addition to reducing carbon emissions, they are also good for the environment in a number of other ways:

- They clean the air and reduce pollution
- They provide shade and help keep built-up areas cool in summer
- They supply the oxygen that we breathe
- They provide habitats for many types of animals
- They prevent flooding by absorbing water from the ground through their roots
- Woods are good places to walk and cycle, and make us feel good

Figure 8.2 Give trees a chance
Source: Anna Loxley

Plantations versus rewilding

Although planting lots of trees seems like a good idea, there are some people who question the way they should be planted. For example, Isabella Tree, the author of *Wilding*, believes that planting large areas of land with similar types of saplings grown artificially in nurseries does not provide the range of healthy trees and other plants needed to support a rich and balanced ecosystem. She believes that nature should be allowed to take its course and land should be given time to regenerate through seed dispersal by birds and wind. For example, jays are known to plant thousands of acorns a month. Regeneration starts with the growth of thorny scrub creating a habitat for a wide variety of wildlife. The scrub also protects saplings that grow through it from animals such as rabbits and deer. It is claimed that trees that have grown naturally are generally healthier than those that are artificially planted, and natural forests are able to capture more carbon dioxide than plantations.

Figure 8.3 Jay with acorn

Green-up outdoor spaces

Gardens provide opportunities to get close to nature and to take action to help combat the climate crisis. Although most gardens are small, added together their effect on the environment can be significant. Collectively, gardens play a crucial role in improving air quality, reducing flooding, moderating climate change, supporting wildlife, and promoting healthy lifestyles.

Many people in cities live in apartments without any garden space, other than their balconies. However, the lack of space on the ground need not prevent us from growing plants, including small trees. In inner-city areas, gardens can be created on rooftops and on the sides of buildings to create 'living roofs' and 'living walls'. The Bosco Verticale (Vertical Forest) is an urban development in Milan, which is renowned for its 'living walls'. The development consists of two tower blocks planted with almost 17,000 trees, shrubs, and plants, which provide greenery equivalent to an area of 20,000 square metres of forest and undergrowth.

Cities are often several degrees warmer than the surrounding countryside. This is due to the buildings trapping heat and the dark paved surfaces absorbing heat from the Sun. This is called the urban 'heat island' effect. If the world climate crisis continues, the 'heat island' effect may make some cities uninhabitable in the summer due to excessively high temperatures and poor air quality. Greening our cities is just as urgent as reforesting rural land, and will not only help reduce carbon emissions, but will also reduce air temperatures, improve air quality, and increase biodiversity.

Figure 8.4 Bosco Verticale

Stop burning fossil fuels

According to the Committee on Climate Change (CCC), most UK homes are not fit for the challenge of the climate crisis. The CCC warns that the UK's climate change targets will

Figure 8.5 Low-carbon home

not be met without the near-complete elimination of greenhouse gas emissions from UK buildings, which in 2019 accounted for 14% of the UK's total emissions.

The replacement of gas boilers with low-carbon technology, such as heat pumps, is a necessary step on the UK's path to becoming a carbon-neutral nation. Making our homes low-carbon and more energy-efficient is action we can take to reduce our carbon footprints. It will also reduce air pollution. The CCC claim that the cost of more efficient heating systems, lighting, appliances, and insulation will be offset by reduced energy bills, which are also likely to fall due to cheap renewable energy becoming more widely available.

Out of the 29 million homes in the UK, only 1 million are heated using low-carbon technology. Most homes use non-renewable forms of energy, which create 14% of the UK greenhouse gas emissions, mostly from gas boilers. Burning natural gas is an example of an irreversible process involving a chemical change. Natural gas is mainly methane, made up of carbon and hydrogen. When burnt in oxygen, it produces carbon dioxide and water and releases large amounts of heat energy.

Methane (carbon & hydrogen) + oxygen = carbon dioxide + water (hydrogen & oxygen) + energy.

Improve home insulation

Whichever way we are thinking of heating our homes, the first thing we should do is to make sure they are well insulated. This will ensure we do not waste energy, and at the same time will minimize our greenhouse emissions. Insulation not only helps keep the home warm in winter, but also keeps it cool in summer. An uninsulated home loses heat through the roof (25%), walls (30%), floors (15%), windows (20%) and draughts (10%). The figures are all approximate, as heat losses vary depending on the construction of the home.

Figure 8.6 Thermal image of heat escaping from house

Blanket insulation, which is made from fibreglass, is commonly used to insulate homes. It is easy to use and is suitable for most areas of the home. As the name implies, fibreglass is made from lots of glass fibres with air trapped in between them. Both glass and air are poor conductors of heat and, when put together, make a good insulating material. Rigid foam is another type of insulation which is often used to insulate new-build homes. It can be used as wall, floor, and roof insulation. Foam is a material in which air or gas bubbles are trapped within a solid or a liquid, making it a good insulator.

Develop low-carbon energy

A vital way to combat the climate crisis is to develop cleaner ways of producing the energy we need. To limit global warming, we need to make better use of low-carbon energy sources such as solar power, wind power, hydropower, tidal power, and nuclear power.

Solar power

Much of the Sun's energy lands on the sea, with only about a third striking the land. However, the energy that can be collected on land has the potential to provide 2,000 times more energy than we presently need. At the moment, we only harness a tiny fraction of the energy the Sun has to offer. However, it is encouraging to know that in the future, solar power has the potential to meet most of our energy needs.

Solar panels are used to collect and convert the Sun's energy into electricity, which is then stored in batteries. As more efficient ways of collecting and storing solar energy are developed, solar power is set to play a major part in reducing greenhouse gas emissions. For example, scientists at Lancaster University in the UK have discovered a way to store solar energy for several years without the need for the electronic equipment in solar panels.

> After studying a type of crystalline material commonly used for desalinating or filtering water, researchers realised it was an extremely effective method of capturing and storing the Sun's energy. The breakthrough paves the way for a whole new range of applications where batteries or other existing technologies are either impractical or too expensive. The material could be used as a coating on buildings to store summer energy that can then be released as heat in the winter, for example. Another potential application, the researchers said, would be as a thin, transparent film on car windows and windshields that could quickly de-ice them on freezing-cold mornings.
>
> (Independent Newspaper, Dec 2020)

Figure 8.7 Solar power plant

Wind power

Wind turbines convert the movement (kinetic) energy of the wind into electricity. The electricity they generate is described as 'clean' because no fossil fuels are burnt in the process. Although they provide clean energy, wind farms can be controversial as local residents find them noisy and they can spoil the aesthetic appeal of the coast and countryside. Building the infrastructure necessary can also damage delicate landscapes and vulnerable wildlife habitats.

Improving technology and lower costs have made wind energy an important alternative to fossil fuels. The UK is one of the best places in the world for wind power, producing 20% of its electricity in 2018. In the last 20 years, the use of wind power has grown exponentially worldwide.

Although wind power can make an important contribution to our energy needs, it does not have anywhere near the same potential as solar energy. This is because much of the wind is inaccessible. It is either too high up in the jet stream or too far out at sea. Even if we turned the whole of the UK into a giant wind farm, we still could not produce enough electricity to meet our future needs.

Hydroelectricity

Gravity plays an important part in the generation of hydroelectricity. Power stations work by storing vast amounts of water in reservoirs, held back by dams. When the water is released, it runs through sloping pipes to turn turbines which generate electricity. Most of Norway's electricity is generated by hydroelectric means; it is also used to generate

Figure 8.8 Offshore wind farm

power in all but two states in the USA. There are a number of hydroelectric power stations in the UK, the largest being the Kielder Power Station in Northumberland.

Hydroelectricity also has its drawbacks. Flooding land for a hydroelectric reservoir can cause extreme damage to rivers, forests, and other wildlife habitats. Agricultural land and scenic countryside can also be destroyed. In many cases, such as the Three Gorges Dam in China, whole communities have had to be relocated.

Hydropower can make an important contribution to our energy needs, but, similar to wind power, it does not have anywhere near the same potential as solar energy. This is because hydropower stations can only be built in places with suitable geography. Today, hydropower provides 16% of the world's electricity, which according to Berners-Lee (2019) could be close to its maximum potential.

Tidal power

Similar to hydropower, gravity plays an important part in tidal power. This is because tides are created by the gravitational pull of the Sun and Moon on the oceans. Using turbines, the movement energy of the tide can be transferred into electrical energy. Tidal power is more reliable and predictable than either wind or solar. However, it is little used at the moment because of the cost and the need for a high tidal movement. The UK, France, Canada, China, and Russia are thought to have the most potential to use this type of energy. Because the technology is still in its infancy, the environmental impact of tidal power stations is largely unknown and the risks to the marine ecosystem need to be better understood.

Nuclear power

Nuclear energy can make a significant contribution to meeting our needs for low-carbon energy, but its use is controversial. Nuclear plants are complicated and slow to build, and hugely expensive compared to wind and solar power. According to Greenpeace, the UK's new Hinkley Point C reactor could cost over £25 billion by the time it is finished, with some people calling it 'the most expensive object on Earth'.

Greenpeace argue that it would be better to spend the money on wind and solar power, which are much quicker to install. There are also extreme risks to public health due to the possibility of accidents and terrorism. Not too long ago, accidents at Chernobyl and Fukushima released huge amounts of radioactive material. Additionally, nuclear waste remains dangerously radioactive for thousands of years and safe storage is a very expensive long-term problem.

Use low-carbon transport

Transport is the biggest source of greenhouse gases in the UK, accounting for about a third of the annual carbon emissions, with vehicles being the largest contributors. Electric vehicles and the electrification of public transport can play a key role in reducing carbon emissions, as well as help to make the air cleaner in towns and cities. Car-sharing and the use of public transport further helps to reduce our carbon footprints. Walking and cycling are basically carbon-free, and also support better health and wellbeing.

Figure 8.9 Tram system in Manchester

Flying has a greater impact on the climate than almost anything else that we do. This is because commercial aircraft use vast amounts of fossil fuels to take off, and while they are flying, they continue to emit greenhouse gases high in the atmosphere, where the gases do most damage. Over the last 20 years, aviation has been one of the fastest-growing contributors to greenhouse gases, and little has been done to reduce its impact on the climate crisis. It has been predicted by the United Nations that aviation could contribute over a quarter of the world's carbon budget by 2050 if decisive action to reduce emissions is not taken. The carbon budget is the maximum amount of carbon that can be emitted into the atmosphere to restrict global warming to 2°C.

There is much ambiguity about what should be done in the shorter term to reduce aviation emissions. The controversial frequent fliers' tax is one possible solution. The majority of flights are taken by businesspeople, who can fly up to 50 times a year. A disincentive to fly could be created by progressively increasing the tax levied on each flight they take over a one-year period. The tax could then be used to offset their emissions.

Develop technologies for carbon capture

Tree planting and rewilding are not the only ways to help control carbon dioxide emissions; technology also has a part to play. Existing technologies are designed to prevent the carbon dioxide produced by burning fossil fuels in power generation and other industries from reaching the atmosphere and contributing to the climate crisis. Firstly, carbon emissions have to be trapped in factory chimneys before they escape. The gas can then be stored deep underground or used to make products such as plastics, fuels, and fertilisers, and to grow greenhouse plants.

New technologies are being developed. For example, the much-loved combination of beer and crisps is being harnessed to tackle climate change. It has been reported that Walkers Crisps has developed a technique that will slash CO_2 emissions from its manufacturing process by 70%. The technology uses potato waste, mixed with CO_2 captured from beer fermentation in a brewery, to produce fertiliser. It will then be used to grow the following year's potato crop. This innovation not only reduces CO_2 emissions from the brewing process, but also reduces the high levels of emissions usually generated by fertilizer manufacture.

Carbon capture is an important technology which has the potential to make a difference. For example, the National Grid suggested that carbon emissions targets from UK's electricity system could be met as early as 2033, if it used carbon capture technology alongside more renewable energy. The technology to capture emissions from factories and power stations is available. However, it is costly and there are no large-scale projects operating in the UK. Another way to capture carbon is to take it straight out of the air, which allows us to undo atmospheric damage. Although nature provides us with trees, marine algae, and other methods to do this job, the technology needed to support nature is yet to be developed.

Offset carbon emissions

Carbon offsetting is a way organisations compensate for their emissions by making carbon dioxide savings elsewhere. Organisations can calculate their carbon footprint by working out their carbon dioxide emissions from all their different activities, including the power they use, ground transport, and air miles. Once they have analysed their carbon footprint, companies buy carbon credits in an offsetting scheme to neutralise the effects of their emissions. The scheme may involve planting trees, investing in reforestation, protecting the Amazon rainforests, or providing low-carbon electricity to developing countries.

Some energy suppliers, who sell energy generated from fossil fuels, use carbon offset schemes to reduce their carbon footprint and to persuade consumers of their 'green credentials'. Offsetting is also a strategy used by the air travel industry. Customers can volunteer to pay a bit more for their travel ticket, for the purpose of reducing their own personal carbon footprint. Only about 1% of passengers take up the option.

Carbon offsetting has its critics. It does not address the primary cause of the climate crisis, which is the massive amount of greenhouse gases being emitted. In fact, it could lead to more emissions with corporations taking less direct action to reduce their carbon footprints, and instead relying on buying more carbon credits. Greenpeace describes carbon offsetting as paying lip service to action, and believes that it does not compare favourably to making frequent fliers pay more heavily for trips abroad.

Choose our future

Now is the time to do what is necessary to ensure the future we want for ourselves and our children, and to prevent the climate crisis causing irreparable damage to our planet. The book 'The Future We Choose' by Christiana Figueres and Tom Rivett-Carnac provides us with contrasting pictures of the world in the year 2050. The first image it presents is of 'The World We Are Creating', in which the climate crisis has continued unabated due to lack of action. This is a world in which some cities are so hot and polluted that people do not go outdoors in the middle of the day, and when they do go out, they wear masks to protect themselves from exhaust fumes from the vast volume of road traffic. This is also a world with a hostile climate where storms, hurricanes, heat waves, and droughts are much more intense and frequent than today. All the summer ice in the Arctic has melted, and due to rising sea levels extreme flooding is commonplace in coastal cities, destroying infrastructure, killing thousands, and displacing millions. This is just a glimpse of the world provided by the authors, where diseases are rampant, people are starving due to highly unpredictable food supplies, and developed countries seal their borders against mass migration. The final picture is of a world in which people are wondering how long the human race can last, and 'how many more generations will see the light of day'.

The second image they provide is of 'The World We Must Create'. This a world in which the climate crisis is a thing of the past and warming has been limited to 1°C. In most places in this world, the air is moist and fresh, even in the cities. Trees are everywhere, and the air is cleaner than before the Industrial Revolution. Cities are healthy and comfortable places to live with many more green spaces and a lot less traffic. Whole streets have been reclaimed for urban agriculture and play areas for children. On every rooftop, people are growing vegetables or flowers, with small urban farms enabling people to source much of their food locally. Outside the cities, rewilding has led to 50% of the world being covered in forests, and more of the agricultural land is used to grow tree-based crops, such as nut and fruit orchards. Most forms of land transport are now electric, with most people choosing to use buses and trams in the city, which are integrated with the high-speed railway system that crisscrosses the rural landscape. This is just a very brief glimpse of the world we must create. It is a world without fossil fuels and greedy self-interest, in which consumerism and profit take a back seat to collective responsibility for the welfare of the planet.

Figure 8.10 Trees growing inside office building

Part 2: Working towards the big idea

This part provides ideas and activities which enable children to work towards understanding the big idea within a framework of good practice. Activities enable children to think, talk, and enquire about actions which we all need to take to help limit global warming to 1.5°C, by reducing our carbon emissions to net zero by 2050. Learning starts by building on children's own understanding of the concept of net zero emissions and the actions necessary to achieve it. Children are encouraged to think critically about the actions we need to take. Finally, children are invited to look into the future to describe the world we are creating due to our lack of action, and compare it with the world we must create to prevent irreparable damage to our planet.

Children have opportunities to develop and use the following science and design technology skills:

- Work collaboratively towards common goals.
- Use different types of scientific enquiries, including data gathering and fair testing.
- Research using secondary sources.
- Generate, develop, model, and communicate ideas through discussion, sketches, and prototypes.
- Communicate outcomes of their research and enquiry in different ways.
- Apply their learning in real-life contexts.

Health and safety

Follow the health and safety guidelines in the ASE publication *'Be Safe!'* when:

- planning the trip to the local park (Studies out of the classroom p12);
- organising a survey of the area around the school (Studies out of the classroom p12);
- making the cool box (Making things p23).

Exploring children's ideas

Start by talking about the Paris Agreement, and how it was agreed to limit warming to less than 2°C and ideally no more than 1.5°C. Scientists believe the 1.5°C target is attainable, but we must cut global greenhouse gas emissions to net zero by 2050 at the latest. Ask children what they understand by net zero emissions and how they think it can be achieved.

Talking points: True, false, or not sure?

- Eating more vegetables and less red meat will increase greenhouse gas emissions.
- What we eat has little effect on greenhouse emissions.

- Trees are nature's way of controlling carbon dioxide emissions.
- We can reduce greenhouse gas emissions to net zero if we stop burning fossil fuels.
- Burning fossil fuels is the only reliable way of producing the energy we need.
- Insulating our homes has no effect on greenhouse gas emissions.
- Insulating our homes saves money on energy bills.
- To reduce greenhouse gas emissions, we need to change the way we heat our homes.
- Driving electric vehicles reduces greenhouse emissions.
- Electric vehicles run on electricity from power stations, which burn fossil fuels.
- Solar power only works in the summer.
- Wind power can produce all the energy we need.

Working in groups, children discuss and respond to the talking points. Groups come together to compare and justify their responses. Talk together about how achieving net zero emissions will require us to change the way we live and work. Ask groups to plan a one-minute presentation which describes how they believe our lives need to change to limit warming to 1.5°C. Compare children's ideas with the actions set out in the first part of this chapter. The models of good practice provide opportunities for children to think and talk about the ideas behind some of the actions that are necessary to combat the climate crisis.

Change our diet

Remind children that methane emitted from cows and sheep is a major greenhouse gas that contributes to the climate crisis. In future, people need to change their diet, and eat more plant-based foods and considerably less red meat. This means restaurants will need to offer environmentally-friendly menus.

Working in groups, children plan an environmentally-friendly menu which offers starters, main courses, and sweets. Groups print their menus on cards and allow members of the class to choose their favourite meals. If the school has appropriate facilities, children can prepare selected dishes from their menus. Debate whether environmentally-friendly restaurants are the thing of the future. Do children think they will be popular with the public? Would their parents or carers like the idea? More activities to do with changing our diet can be found in the next chapter.

Plant more trees

Clarify what is meant by net zero emissions. Point out that to achieve net zero we not only need to reduce the amount of greenhouse gases we put into the air, but we also need to take out of the air the equivalent amount of carbon we put into it. Introduce the term 'sequestration', to mean removing and storing excess carbon dioxide from the air. Describe trees as nature's way of controlling the amount of carbon dioxide in the air, and talk about other advantages trees provide for the environment. Relevant information can be found in Part 1.

Enquire! Re-envisioning the local park

Introduce children to the idea that we need to think about our world differently in order to tackle the climate crisis. For example, we need to think of green spaces, such as parks, as places which have an important part to play in controlling the amount of carbon dioxide in the air. This may require our parks to be redesigned to maximise their potential for carbon sequestration. Talk about tree planting as a simple and effective way to sequester carbon. Discuss how it can improve biodiversity and at the same time make our towns and cities cleaner and more beautiful places.

Plan a trip to the local park to explore its potential to capture and lock up carbon. Children design their own data sheets for their survey to record the different types and numbers of trees and shrubs. They also draw plans of the park showing areas of vegetation, including grassed areas, and areas set aside for leisure, sporting activities, and parking. Children record specific details using sketches and photographs.

Back in school, children work in groups to redesign the park to maximise its potential to remove carbon dioxide from the air. To help with their design, children use the web to explore the best carbon-storing trees that are commonly found in the UK, and decide on the ones which are suitable for their area. Redesigning the park requires children to reimagine how people will use it. Because trees are such good carbon sinks, children may need to think about replacing areas of grass and bedding plants with mixed woodland. Encourage debate about whether we need to convert our parks into woodland to help achieve net zero and also protect wildlife. Groups produce plans for the local park, and explain how they envisage it being used by people in the future. If appropriate, they can use the outcomes of their enquiry to appeal to their local council to improve the park. They should present their evidence and recommendations in a formal report.

Figure 8.11 Should parks be turned into woodland?

Green-up outdoor spaces

Parks are not the only spaces in our towns and cities where trees and other plants can be grown to capture carbon and improve the environment. Gardens may individually only provide space for a small number of trees and other plants, but collectively they can make a major contribution to combating the climate crisis. Children debate whether the government should provide advice to people about what to grow in their gardens as part of their policy on climate change. Talk together about the best advice the government could provide. If the climate crisis gets worse, should the government advice be made compulsory? Debate whether people should be told what to grow in their gardens.

Talk about growing plants in our streets. Debate whether there should be more trees planted in our streets. Organise the children to survey the area within a few minutes' walk around your school, and estimate the number of trees which could be planted in the streets. Draw plans of the area which include existing trees and sites where more trees could be planted. Publish the outcome of the survey on the school website or the school's social media platform. If appropriate, children can write to the local council to enquire whether more trees should be planted. Based on the outcome of their survey, children can use local maps to very roughly estimate the number of extra trees which could be planted in a square mile around your school, and then scale up for the number for trees which could be planted in your town or city. How big would a forest have to be to include all these trees?

Design! Roof top gardens and living walls

Start by showing children pictures of the Bosco Verticale, Milan. Talk about the concepts of 'living walls'. Working in groups, children use information sources to discover how

Figure 8.12 Vertical garden in Paris

the Bosco Verticale was developed, and which types of trees were chosen based on their ability to survive in containers and in hot and windy conditions. Groups can also explore 'living wall' and 'roof top gardens' in the UK and in other parts of the world.

Working in groups, children design and create a 'living model' of a city centre building planned to help combat the climate crisis. The building should be designed to be used by people for either work, leisure, or to live in. Children build the model from any suitable materials available in school, and must use real plants for 'living walls' and 'roof top gardens'. When designing the building, they should incorporate a watering system for the plants. They can use easy-to-grow grasses or succulents to represent trees and shrubs. Children should be reminded that areas of ground around the building are also part of the development and should be put to good agricultural or horticultural use in their model. Talk about whether buildings of the future could be designed so people can grow their own food and provide their own energy.

Stop burning fossil fuels

Start by pointing out that most of us in the UK use fossil fuels to heat our homes, which create 14% of our greenhouse gas emissions, mostly from gas boilers.

Ask children what type of energy they would choose to power their 'living' building. Talk about the need to replace fossils fuels with low-carbon alternatives, such as:

- Solar power
- Wind power
- Hydro power
- Tidal power
- Nuclear power

Working in groups, children use information sources to identify the advantages and disadvantages of each of these low-carbon energy sources. Children should consider cost and environmental issues, as well as the potential to reduce greenhouse gases. Groups present their findings to the rest of the class and make an argument for the two low-carbon sources which can contribute most to combating the climate crisis.

To provide its own energy, their 'living' building would need to be powered by either solar or wind energy. Discuss which source children think would be most suitable for their building. Groups can add solar panels (cells) to their model and wire them so they light up parts of the building. As a D&T project, they could also make model wind generators. Information for how to make the models can be found on the web.

Storytelling! Transport in the year 2121

Ask children to describe what they understand about the transport system in the UK. How does this differ to other transport system around the world? Transport systems can include roads, railways, tramways, seaways, and airways. Working in groups, children debate how the UK's transport system will need to change to help reduce greenhouse emissions to net zero.

Challenge groups to design a transport system which is fit for a pollution-free world in the 22nd century. Focus their attention on the use of privately owned vehicles, such as motor cars. As the population increases, is it feasible to keep building more and more motor vehicles for individual use? More cars and lorries require more roads, leading to the destruction of already endangered wildlife habitats to make room for them. How many motor vehicles can we drive in our cities before total gridlock? Ask children to use their imaginations to design a future transport system which relies less on privately owned vehicles and more on public transport. Also, encourage them to research the development of carbon-free passenger aircraft for long-distance travel. Groups present and justify their ideas to the class, and describe how families in 2121 would travel to school and work, do their shopping, and go on holiday. Debate how people's lives may have to change for the health of the planet.

Enquire! Home insulation

Remind children that designing a low-carbon home is not just about using low-carbon sources of energy for lighting and heating. The house should also be well-insulated to prevent heat being wasted. Insulation not only helps keep the home warm in winter, but also keeps it cool in summer.

Figure 8.13 Wall insulation
Source: Anna Loxley

Start by showing children a picture of a house and ask them to identify all the ways heat can escape in winter. Talk about how we can prevent heat escaping. Focus on each part of the house in turn. Use pictures from the web to illustrate how double-glazing works, and how other types of insulation are used in the home. Talk about how most insulation materials have air trapped inside them to help prevent heat escaping. Link these ideas to the work you do on properties of materials.

To investigate the insulating properties of materials, set children a challenge to design and build a cool box to prevent an ice balloon from melting. The containers which use the least amount of insulating materials and keep the ice solid for the longest time are the most efficient. Provide groups with a variety of insulation materials which they can test to help them choose the best materials. Emphasise that children need to control their tests to make sure the comparisons are fair. Compare the performance of the children's boxes with commercially made coolers.

Information sources

Websites

- A new British electric aircraft (aerosociety.com)
- Can planting billions of trees save the planet? | World news | The Guardian
- Carbon Farming: Sequestering Carbon in Plants and Soil – ethical.net
- Electric flight – Zero emission – Airbus
- Fossil fuels and climate change: the facts | ClientEarth
- Gardening for Climate Change | National Wildlife Federation (nwf.org)
- Grow your own forest: how to plant trees to help save the planet | Trees and forests | The Guardian
- Introduction to Green Roof Benefits (livingroofs.org)
- Nuclear power | Greenpeace UK
- The Green Roof Centre | Landscape | The University of Sheffield
- Tidal energy | National Geographic Society
- What Is A Solar Panel? How does a solar panel work? (mrsolar.com)
- UK firm's solar power breakthrough could make world's most efficient panels by 2021 | Manufacturing sector | The Guardian

Working on scientific understanding

In this part, children work on their understanding of how trees and other plants capture and store carbon dioxide from the air. Link this part with your curriculum work on plants.

Start by using illustrations and/or animations to talk about how plants (trees) produce their own carbon-based food. Describe the leaves as food-making machines in which the ingredients, carbon dioxide from the air, and water and nutrients from the soil are mixed together. Light energy from the Sun is then used to 'cook up' the ingredients to make carbon-based materials (carbohydrates) which the plant uses to grow. Therefore, the carbon dioxide that plants use to grow ends up stored in the structure of the plants.

Carbon dioxide + water + light energy = carbon-based materials + oxygen.

Enquire! Plant anatomy

Working in groups, children observe different types of leaves in detail using hand-lenses and microscopes. Ask them to accurately sketch the structure, clearly showing the holes (stoma) through which carbon dioxide gets into the leaves. Use animations from video clips on the web to help children visualise how a plant takes in water and nutrients through its roots, and how its leaves take in carbon dioxide and absorb light energy. Talk about how trees release oxygen and water vapour through their leaves back into the air. Point out how trees not only sequester carbon dioxide, but also provide vital oxygen for us and other animals to breathe. Also describe how the water vapour trees release has a cooling effect on the environment.

Enquire! Rewilding

Environmentalists such as Isabella Tree, the author of *Wilding*, believe that nature should be allowed to take its course, and rather than us planting trees on waste ground, the land should be given time to regenerate through seed dispersal by birds and wind.

Talk together about the different ways native trees disperse their seeds. List the seeds that are dispersed by wind and those by animals. What other ways do trees disperse their seeds? Working in groups, children discuss whether they think the natural regeneration of wasteland is a feasible way of tackling the climate crisis. Is there enough time to let nature take its course, or do we need to give it a helping hand?

If you have space, in autumn clear a small area of school ground to explore how quickly regeneration takes place. Work the ground to make it suitable for growing shrubs and trees, then let nature take its course for the next twelve months. Each month, children identify new plants and record the numbers of each species in a bar graph. At the start, children speculate about which types of plants they expect to find growing in the plot. Ask children to provide reasons for their ideas. Which trees are most likely to find a home there? In spring, as plants start to grow, set up a webcam to monitor the wildlife that visits the plot, including birds, butterflies, bees, bats, hedgehogs, mice, and any other creature in search of shelter or a meal. At the end of the year, children use their findings to publish a report on the biodiversity of the plot, and draw conclusions about the benefits of regeneration. Monitor the long-term development of the rewilding plot by making it a project for different groups year after year.

Develop carbon capture technologies

Talk about how we cannot rely on tree planting and rewilding to solve the climate crisis on their own. To reduce UK emissions to net zero, we need to develop technologies to capture and store emissions as they are produced in power stations and factories, before they get into the air. Talk about the problems with storage. Ask children what they think happens to all the carbon dioxide which is collected. Where can it be stored? How can it be used? Talk about how Walkers Crisps use CO2 emissions to produce fertilizer to grow their potatoes. Information is provided in Part 1.

Working in groups, children design their own solution to make use of captured carbon dioxide. They should start by using information sources to research the many industrial uses of carbon dioxide, including drinks and food, medicine, fertilizers, plastics, horticulture, and others. Encourage children to use their imaginations to design novel ways of using the gas in new products. Groups create posters to advertise how their products are environmentally friendly.

Information sources

Websites

- Beer and crisps used to help tackle climate change – BBC News
- Green Flying Duty. Responsible Travel.
- Home – TreeSisters
- Researchers discover material can store solar energy for years | The Independent
- Turning carbon dioxide into cash – BBC News
- What is carbon capture, usage and storage – and can it trap emissions? | Carbon capture and storage (CCS) | The Guardian
- What is carbon offsetting? | World Economic Forum (weforum.org)

The bigger picture

Choose our future

This part encourages children to choose their future by imagining what the world will be like in 2050 if the climate crisis continues out of control, and comparing that world with one in which emissions have been reduced to net zero and global warming limited to 1.5°C. We start with the weather forecast.

World weather forecast for 2050

Start this activity by showing children the Met Office video *Future weather forecast 2050*. Discuss what the extremes of weather could be like by 2050 if global warming continues out of control. Extremes of weather include heat waves, droughts, tropical storms, extensive flooding, and extreme hurricanes. Summer temperatures in the UK could regularly rise above 40°C, with many vulnerable people unable to go out during the day. With emissions out of control, air quality at times may be so poor that people with respiratory problems cannot leave their homes. Children use information sources to help them picture the impact of the climate crisis in 2050.

Working in groups, children use their understanding of the climate crisis to produce a possible weather forecast for 2050. They present their forecast in the form of an app which is targeted at a particular end-user. The app should have an opening page designed to grab the user's attention and then another page which presents a seven-day weather forecast focused on the needs and interests of the user. For example, the app could be targeted at farmers, gardeners, travel agents, or fishermen. It could be designed especially for older people or people in poor health who are worried about going out in extreme weather. Children use their imaginations and think about who in society would benefit from the app in times of highly volatile weather. The app should be easy to use and include its own set of signs, symbols, and pictograms that children think would appeal to the user.

Story-telling! Two worlds

Introduce children to the book 'The Future We Choose' by Christiana Figueres and Tom Rivett-Carnac. Talk briefly about the contrasting pictures it provides of the world in the year 2050. More information can be found in Part 1.

Working in groups, children use their imagination and their understanding of the climate crisis to produce two contrasting descriptions of the world in 2050. The first describes what the world would be like if the climate crisis continues out of control. The second describes a world in 2050 with greenhouse emissions reduced to net zero and average temperatures limited to 1.5°C above pre-industrial levels. Use the stories to promote a debate about the possible future children will inherit.

Design! Future living

Working in groups, children design and create plans for low-carbon living in the future, which produces a negative carbon footprint; in other words, our way of living removes more carbon from the air than it puts into it.

For this activity, children need to be clear that they are designing a model lifestyle for the future, beyond 2050. The climate crisis is over, but we still need to reduce the amount of greenhouses gases in the air. The first thing children need to do is to design a home which has a negative footprint. Talk about how designing a low-carbon home is not just about using low-carbon energy sources. Everything to do with the home, especially its situation and layout, needs to be considered. For example, children should design the home to take maximum advantage of the available sunshine. This involves the way the house is situated and the way the windows are designed; rooms used during the day need to have the most natural light. Encourage them to think about installing a heat-pump and solar panels. The use of solar panels can contribute carbon-free energy to the national grid. Also, the design of the outdoor space is crucial to reduce the carbon footprint.

When designing a future way of living, children should consider how people will get about. What transport will they use on local journeys for work, school, and shopping?

Figure 8.14 Low-carbon living

Figure 8.15 The future we choose!

And what about longer journeys, such as holidays abroad? What will they do about consumer products such as food, clothes, and electrical goods to reduce their footprint? Encourage debate about consumerism. Would they be prepared to pay more for locally produced goods, or even produce their own when possible?

Groups set out their ideas for future living on posters, which include town planning ideas to achieve a negative carbon footprint. Posters can be exchanged with other groups. As the posters circulate, groups evaluate each other's ideas and add comments on sticky notes. Groups come together and use the ideas on the sticky notes as the basis for discussion. Finish the activity with each group being given one minute to summarise how our lives need to change to solve the climate crisis.

Information sources

Websites

- Future Visions of Our Planet | WWF
- Future weather forecast for the year 2050 – Met Office
- How the World Will Look if We Don't Address Climate Change | Time
- What would a climate-friendly UK mean for you? | Climate change | The Guardian

Books

- Berners-Lee, M. (2019) *There Is No Planet B*. Cambridge: Cambridge University Press.
- Figueres, C. and Rivett-Carnac, T. (2021) *The Future We Choose*. London: Manilla Press.

CHAPTER 9

TAKING CLIMATE ACTION

Big Idea: *We need to change the way we live in order to reduce carbon emissions to net zero and prevent irreparable damage to our planet.*

   This chapter provides opportunities for children to develop their understanding of some of the actions they personally can take to reduce their carbon footprint. Part 1 starts by describing some of the things young activists around the world are doing to help address the climate crisis, and then goes on to discuss actions that children can take.

Topics include:

- Meet Generation Greta: young climate activists around the world
- Eco-anxiety
- Getting to know our carbon footprint
- Eat for your health and that of the planet
- Cut down on waste
- Green-up the school
- Get involved with citizen science

Part 1: Subject knowledge

Meet Generation Greta: young climate activists around the world

They are too young to vote, but schoolchildren across the globe have been taking matters into their own hands, ever since Greta Thunberg started the Future for Friday (FFF) climate strikes to protest the lack of action by governments in combatting the climate crisis. In 2019, more than 1.5 million young people in more than 125 countries walked out of schools, colleges, and universities in the biggest day of global climate action ever.

The urgency of their protests reflects the very narrow window of opportunity left to make positive change. We are already living outside the climate parameters that first gave rise to humans, and the world's leading climate scientists agree that we have only 12 years to limit global warming to a maximum of 1.5°C. Still, most governments are not doing enough to stay within these limits as set out by the United Nation's 2015 Paris Agreement.

(The Guardian Newspaper, June, 2019)

Climate activists around the world have shown that young people can make a significant contribution to combating the climate crisis. Greta Thunberg is still probably the best-known young activist, but there are many others of her generation who work enthusiastically to improve the environment and protect wildlife where they live. Here are just a few examples of what remarkable things they can achieve:

Yola Mgogwana lives in Cape Town, South Africa

Yola Mgogwana was 11 years old when she first became a climate activist. On Friday 15th March 2019, Yola led children in her primary school in the 'Future for Friday' strike to protest against the lack of action by her government to combat the climate crisis. Her story was published in the Guardian newspaper, where she voiced her enthusiasm for young people to get involved:

Because I believe in youth using their voice for change, I was selected as Chair Lady for our Club. When Future for Friday Africa approached our club to get involved, it was an immediate 'Yes'! I knew I needed to represent the voices of black youth from under resourced communities in Cape Town. I was happy when I got chosen as one of the speakers at the main event.

Yola also volunteered to take part in the Earthchild Project, which integrates environmental education into classrooms and communities. She believes that every school should make environmental education part of their curriculum. From the impoverished township in which she lives, Yola sees the effects of the climate crisis everyday:

"Our weather is not normal – one day it is hot, the next day it's raining heavily. It's a huge problem for farmers, and mudslides wash away houses, leaving poor families without homes."

Amy and Ella Meek live in Nottinghamshire, UK

Teenage sisters Amy and Ella Meek are passionate about reducing the use of single-use plastics. To get things done, they founded 'Kids Against Plastic,' a charity set up by kids, for kids. As it says on the website, 'Kids Against Plastic' is all about taking action against plastic pollution. Speaking to a Guardian newspaper journalist, Amy advocated that the school curriculum should be more focused on environmental issues:

'Kids can have a really powerful voice when they find something they are passionate about – but the key is to be educated about it in the first place,' argues Amy, who wishes the school curriculum focused more on environmental issues . . . 'The wasteful production of single-use plastics is so interconnected with the consumption of fossil fuels and global warming, and learning about these problems really opened our eyes,' Amy says.

Holly Gillibrand lives in Lochaber, Scotland

Holly Gillibrand is a well-known youth climate activist and rewilding campaigner. She is part of the global movement known as 'Schools 4 Climate Action', and was named as the Young Scotswoman of the Year by the by the Glasgow Times newspaper. In 2019, Holly was named on the prestigious Woman's Hour Power List, which celebrates the significant contributions women are making to the protection of the environment and the sustainability of our planet. In 2020, she supported presenter Chris Packham in a national campaign to end wildlife crime, and is a youth advisor and 'future voice' for the charity Heal Rewilding, which aims to return more land to nature in the fight against climate change.

Like fellow youth campaigners, Holly believes governments are not doing enough to combat the climate crisis, and more action is needed:

> Change has to start with the governments, we need to have politicians who have an appetite for change, rather than just wanting to prop up the status quo. It's not enough to care about it, we have to take action and do something about it.

Holly's story was published in the Glasgow Times in December 2020.

Lilly Platt lives in Zeist, in the Netherlands

Lilly's activism started at the age of 6 after seeing the astonishing amount of plastic litter on a walk with her grandfather. Soon after, she started her own clean-up campaign, which has since grown through social media to become known as 'Lilly's Plastic Pickup'.

Like other climate activists, Lilly's main goal is to persuade global politicians and policymakers to take action to mitigate the harmful effects of climate change and plastic pollution. She has received several awards for her environmental work, including a 'Lijntje' award for Outstanding Achievement and an International Eco Hero Award. She is also a Global Youth Ambassador for Earth.Org, and tells the following story about the reasons she became an activist:

> Back in 2014, when I was 6 years old, me and my grandfather were walking and we saw piles of plastic that had been thrown everywhere: on the roads, on the grass- so we decided it would be a good idea to count the pieces of plastic and after at least 10/15 minutes of walking, we found 91 pieces of plastic. I was shocked! I found out that it would eventually make its way into the ocean and become part of the "plastic soup" and it was at that moment that I realised that I had to do something about it.

Eco-anxiety

'Adults keep saying, we owe it to the young people to give them hope. But I don't want your hope, I don't want you to be hopeful, I want you to panic'. These are the words of Greta Thunberg when talking about the need for more action to combat the climate crisis. Although we can understand the sense of urgency she is trying to convey, the last thing we want to do in our schools is to instil a sense of panic in our children about the future.

According to reports in the press, there is evidence that some people are indeed panicking, due to feeling overwhelmed and powerless in the face of what they see as an imminent and unstoppable global disaster. Levels of alarm are growing and have led to the phenomenon of 'eco-anxiety', which has been described as a psychological disorder afflicting a growing number of people who worry about the climate crisis.

To avoid causing anxiety, we need to get the message across to children that there are many people working hard to solve the climate problems, including many young people like themselves. We should point out that there are positive solutions to the crisis, including the new technologies explored in the previous chapter, and there are also things they can do to help shape our future in a positive way.

Getting to know our carbon footprint

As Greta Thunberg often reminds us, we should be following and acting on the science. It's the scientists we should be listening to before deciding what actions we can take to help combat the climate crisis. Children need reliable knowledge and good role models to recognise their own environmental impacts and to be persuaded to change their behaviours towards more sustainable lifestyles. Youth activists, like Amy and Ella Meek, were persuaded to take climate action because environmental education at school opened their eyes to the damage that their everyday actions were causing to the planet.

The first thing children need to understand is that nearly all their actions contribute to the climate crisis in either a positive or negative way. Actions that have the potential to reduce their carbon footprints contribute in a positive way, and things they do that increase their carbon footprints contribute to making the crisis worse. Everyone's footprint is different, and it is a good idea for children to know what theirs looks like to help them decide what action they can take to help tackle the climate crisis.

Our carbon footprints provide a measure of the amount of greenhouse gases that our activities produce each year. The convention is to express a carbon footprint in terms of the carbon dioxide equivalent (CO_2e) of all the greenhouse gases that are produced by the activity in question. For example, the manufacture of an ice cream causes methane (from the cows), carbon dioxide (from manufacture and transport) and nitrous oxide (from farming) to be released into the air. Rather than write out a list of the quantities of these different greenhouse gases, the carbon footprint is expressed in an equivalent amount of carbon dioxide, approximately 500g CO_2e, which includes a flake from an ice cream van. This figure represents the total impact that eating an ice-cream has on the climate crisis. Compare this to taking a bath heated by solar energy (200g CO_2e), and we can see that enjoying an ice cream is not particularly environmentally friendly. Here are some other examples of carbon footprints taken from Berners-Lee (2019):

- Enjoying a banana (110g CO2e)
- Boiling a litre of water using an electric kettle (170g CO2e)
- Travelling a mile on a London bus (half full) (46g CO2e)
- Travelling for a mile in second class on an intercity train (80g CO2e)
- Enjoying a cheeseburger (3.2kg CO2e)
- A pair of all-leather shoes (15Kg CO2e)
- Travelling a mile by car on congested roads (16Kg CO2e)
- Manufacture and lifetime wear of a pair of jeans (32Kg CO2e)
- Sunday roast leg of lamb 2kg weight (42kg CO2e)
- Using a smartphone 3 hours a day (69kg CO2e)
- Owning an average-sized pet dog for a year (770kg CO2e)

Actions children can take to reduce their carbon footprint

Reducing their carbon footprint may prove challenging for children, since much of what they do is influenced by the lifestyle of their family. However, as the work of young activists around the world demonstrates, there is always something children can do if they are made aware of how their actions impact the health of the planet. The following provides the background to actions which children should know about. School activities based on these actions are set out in Part 2.

Eat for your health and that of the planet

One of the biggest challenges in reducing our carbon footprint is changing our diets. However, the good news is that healthy eating is not only good for the children; it is also good for the planet because it can help reduce our carbon footprint. Food is a basic need and children are not able to directly influence how it is produced, kept fresh, and transported. However, they can indirectly influence how foods are produced and transported by choosing to eat foods with relatively low carbon footprints. Supermarkets are sensitive to customer demands. If the demand is big enough, supermarkets in time will stock those foods that do less damage to the environment.

In Part 2, children are encouraged to speculate about how the food they eat contributes to their carbon footprints. For example, a cheese sandwich involves growing wheat, harvesting and transporting the grain, making the bread, packaging and transporting it to the supermarket, lighting and heating the supermarket, shopping, and waste. All these processes produce greenhouse gas emissions which add to the children's carbon footprints. We also have to add the emissions due to the production of the cheese. By developing an awareness of all the processes that contribute to greenhouse gases, children can make informed decisions about which products to buy based on where and how they are produced.

Figure 9.1 Plant to plate

Eat less meat

Previous chapters outline how the foods we eat contribute to the climate crisis. To reduce our carbon footprint, the Intergovernmental Panel on Climate Change (IPCC) recommends that people eat a lot less meat, especially pork and beef, and eat more plant-based foods. The recommendation means that some people will be asked to reduce their meat consumption by 77% and their consumption of dairy products by 40%. The Climate Change Committee (CCC) plan is less radical, requiring a reduction in meat eating of 20% by 2030, and 35% by 2050. Public sector caterers serving billions of meals a year in UK schools, universities, hospitals, and care homes pledged to cut the amount of meat they serve by 20%, the equivalent of 45,000 cows a year. The CCC said action to cut food waste by 50% by 2030 is also needed.

Choose a balanced diet

One of the ways the WWF is helping children reduce their carbon footprints is through their *Plant2Plate Campaign for Schools*. The campaign focusses on what can be done to produce and consume food in a sustainable way that is less harmful to the planet and healthier for the children. Full details of the campaign, with lots of resources for schools, can be found on their Plant2Plate web pages.

Six Livewell principles for healthy and sustainable food:

- Eat more plants, and enjoy vegetables and wholegrains.
- Eat a variety of foods, and have a colourful plate.

- Waste less food. One third of food produced for human consumption is lost or wasted.
- Moderate your meat consumption, red and white, and instead enjoy other sources of proteins such as peas, beans, and nuts.
- Buy food that meets a credible certified standard, such as the Marine Stewardship Council (MSC), free-range, and fair trade.
- Eat fewer foods high in fat, salt, and sugar and keep foods such as cakes, sweets and chocolate, cured meat, chips, and crisps to an occasional treat. Choose water, avoid sugary drinks, and remember that juices only count as one of your five a day, however much you drink.

(WWF Livewell website)

Cut down on waste

About 7 million tonnes of food are thrown away by households in the UK every year, which amounts to each family throwing away £700 worth of shopping. Much of this food ends up rotting in landfill sites, where it releases methane into the atmosphere. In some authorities, food waste is collected separately from general waste, and used to produce biogas to generate electricity and heat homes. A further by-product of the process is bio-fertiliser, which is rich in nutrients such as nitrogen, potassium, and other elements required for healthy plant growth and fertile soil.

Much of our food waste can also be composted at home, along with the garden waste. Only vegetable waste should be added to a normal compost bin. Composting our waste produces less methane than the landfill. This is because the food decomposes in a different way, involving types of bacteria which do not produce methane. According to Recycle Now, the average primary school produces 45kg of waste per child each year, most of which is food, paper, or card. Most of this waste can easily be recycled or composted.

Cut down on single-use plastics

Plastics generate heat-trapping gases at every stage of their life cycle, according to a newsletter published by Yale University. We all know the impact plastics have had on marine animals, but that is only part of the pollution story. Plastics are made from fossil fuels and billions of tonnes of greenhouse gases are emitted through their extraction, transportation, manufacture, recycling, and incineration.

> Today, about 4–8% of annual global oil consumption is associated with plastics, according to the World Economic Forum. If this reliance on plastics persists, plastics will account for 20% of oil consumption by 2050.
>
> Yale Climate Connections, August 2019

This plastic binge means that by 2050 plastic will be responsible for up to 13% of the total "carbon budget" set out in the Paris Climate Agreement, which is equivalent to the emissions from 615 coal-fired power plants. About half of the billions of plastic products around the world are single-use, and only a small percentage of them are recycled. Conservationists worldwide are calling for a move towards 'zero waste' regarding plastics. This means the development of low-carbon production methods and more responsible consumption, reuse, and recycling of materials, without incineration or landfilling.

Green-up the school

As discussed in the previous chapter, plants are nature's way of sequestering carbon dioxide from the air. Gardens also improve air quality, support wildlife, and are good for children's physical and mental development. Schools which have space the size of a tennis court can plant a mini forest school classroom or a peaceful spot that is an oasis for birds, as well as a 'factory' for sequestering carbon dioxide. Refer to the Woodland Trust website (Free Trees for Schools) for information about the best trees to plant.

If space is limited, schools can plant small varieties of fruit trees in containers, and grow woody climbers and shrubs up fences and walls. Planting long-lived shrubs is better for the environment than herbaceous annuals which capture less carbon. Growing vegetables is another good way to capture carbon, and it also helps reduce food miles and plastic waste which are all part of the school's carbon footprint. No matter how much schools are able to grow, every lettuce, tomato, or courgette contributes to the fight against climate change. Growing vegetables also provides opportunities to make good use of composted waste.

Figure 9.2 Every little bit helps

Create a butterfly garden

Insects have been particularly hard hit by the climate crisis, and creating a butterfly garden can help save them, as well as sequestering carbon from the air. Butterflies have been very badly affected, with three-quarters of the 56 species of British butterflies in decline. Butterflies are a bit like Goldilocks, preferring conditions to be neither too hot nor too cold, but "just right". They are highly sensitive to the rhythms of the seasonal temperatures to trigger reproduction, migration, and hibernation. Also, they are cold-blooded and rely on heat from the Sun to warm their bodies. This makes them vulnerable to climate change.

Butterflies feed on nectar to gain the energy to keep active in spring and autumn. In spring, they need energy to fly and mate after their winter hibernation, and in autumn nectar enables them to build up reserves of energy to get them through the winter hibernation. Migrant butterflies, such as the Painted Lady, need to build up reserves of energy to make their long journey back to North Africa. In 2021, Butterfly Conservation ran a project to map the arrival of the Painted Lady and other migrant insects to find out whether climate change is having an impact on the numbers visiting the UK. Visit their website to obtain up-to-date information.

Get involved with citizen science

> Thanks to the dedication and expertise of many thousands of volunteers working closely with the professionals we are now able to document even more about the changing state of nature across our land and in our seas.
>
> Sir David Attenborough

Science education should be relevant to children's lives, and what could be more relevant than helping them take part in real scientific research? Citizen science lets children get involved by collecting or analysing existing data and uploading the results. The results can contribute to the success of national and international research projects about the effects of climate change. Children benefit because they develop more scientific knowledge and skills, and at the same time gain the satisfaction of knowing they have been involved in real and important scientific research.

Mass participation projects enable scientists to collect huge amounts of data which, without the help of the public, would not be possible. For example, the Woodland Trust's Nature's Calendar project asked children to record clues that suggested seasonal changes. They were asked to record when they saw birds nesting, migrating, and the flowering of certain plants. This type of information can help scientists explore the effects climate change and weather patterns might be having on the seasonal behaviour of wildlife. The Big Garden Birdwatch is a longstanding citizen science project organised by RSPB. The large size of the survey allows scientists to monitor the numbers of the different species of birds which visit our gardens and, by comparing them with previous years, to work out how the climate crisis and other changes to their environment may be impacting them.

The European Commission believes that changes in children's behaviours towards more sustainable lifestyles can happen through direct involvement in citizen science projects, because they can observe and monitor their own environmental impacts.

It is essential to directly involve citizens and communities in contributing to climate action and protecting the environment, thereby encouraging them to change their personal behaviour, reducing their carbon and environmental footprint and taking action at the individual and collective level.

(European Commission)

Through these projects, children can become ambassadors for climate action and environmental protection by sharing their knowledge and experience with their families, friends, and communities.

Part 2: Working towards the big idea

This part provides ideas and activities which enable children to work towards understanding the big idea within a framework of good practice. The activities enable children to learn about actions they can take to reduce their carbon emissions and help prevent irreparable damage to our planet. Progression towards the big idea starts by children exploring the nature of the school's carbon emissions, and by providing an action plan to reduce them. Children also work on their understanding of the nature of their own carbon footprint and explore ways to reduce it. As part of the bigger picture, they apply their understanding of carbon sequestration by choosing plants to green-up the school to support local wildlife and to reduce their carbon footprints. Opportunities are also provided for children to engage with relevant citizen science projects.

Health and safety

Follow the health and safety codes in the ASE publication *'Be Safe!'* when:

- composting waste and planting trees and other plants (Gardening p14);
- planning a trip to the recycling plant and organising citizen science projects (Studies outside the classroom p12);
- making patchwork products (Making things p23)

Exploring children's ideas

Young climate activists

Talk to children about the work of climate activists such as Greta Thunberg, Yola Mgogwana, Amy and Ella Meek, Holly Gillibrand, and Lilly Platt. Refer to Part 1.

Working in groups, children use information sources to explore the work of young climate activists around the world. Groups come together to share and discuss their findings and talk about what they can do to mitigate climate change and reduce plastic pollution. Produce and display poster profiles about each young activist.

Mini COP conference

Talk about how heads of state, climate experts, and campaigners from around the world meet every year to agree on coordinated action to tackle the climate crisis. Point out that the meetings are known as Conferences of the Parties (COP). In 2021, the 26th meeting (COP 26) was held in Glasgow. Use information from Chapter 1 to discuss the outcomes of this meeting. Children can research the outcomes of other conferences since 2021 on the web. Remind children of all the positive things people are doing to address climate change, and talk about the new technologies which are being developed which will make the environment cleaner and life better in the future. (Refer to Chapter 8 for relevant information).

Suggest children hold their own climate change conference to agree on what the school community can do to help address the climate crisis. Start the conference by discussing the school's main sources of greenhouse gas emissions. Focus on school meals, sources of energy, types of waste, single-use plastics, and transport. Background knowledge is provided in previous chapters.

Conference breaks up into groups to discuss what the school can do to reduce its carbon footprint. Groups present their ideas to conference and justify why the actions provide practical ways to reduce the school's footprint. Focus discussion on how they can persuade decision-makers in the school community to put the actions into practice. Conference chooses the actions which they believe will be most effective and discuss a plan to publicise and implement them. An action plan could include policies on the following:

- School catering (policy to use less red meat and dairy, and to prioritise the use of locally produced food)
- Use of school grounds and buildings (policy to green-up the school for carbon sequestration and to reduce food miles by growing its own vegetables)
- Travel and transport (policy which encourages walking, cycling, and use of public and low-carbon transport. Also, no-idling zones around the school)
- Sources of energy (policy to use clean energy)
- Save energy (policy to prevent the loss of energy through school infrastructure)
- Use of plastics (policy which bans single-use plastics and seeks to use products made from sustainable materials)
- Compost, recycle, reuse, and repurpose (policy to compost food, used paper and garden waste, and to recycle, reuse, or repurpose products made from materials such as glass, metal, fabric, and wood)

To put their plan into action, children need to first persuade the head teacher and the school governors that what they propose is worthwhile. They may also want to campaign for the support of local businesses who can provide practical help, materials, and advice. By making the campaign public on social media and in local newspapers, the school provides a positive model for the wider community, which can inspire them to take similar action to address the biggest issue of our time. Start the campaign by publishing the children's top ten tips for reducing carbon emissions on the school's website.

Figure 9.3 Solar panel parking

Actions children can take to reduce their carbon footprint

Activities in the rest of this chapter provide opportunities for children to explore how they can reduce their own carbon footprints.

Cut down on waste

Show children a picture of a landfill site. What comes into the children's minds? Do they know what types of materials are put in landfill? In groups, children discuss materials which they think are put into landfill and those which are recycled. Here are some facts about landfill to share with the children:

- On average every person in the UK throws away their own body weight in rubbish every 7 weeks. In less than 2 hours, the UK could fill the Albert Hall with its waste.
- 8 million nappies are thrown away every day.
- 7 million trees are cut down each year to make disposable nappies.
- It is estimated that as much as 80% of the contents of our general waste wheelie bin could have been recycled or composted.
- Each year in the UK, we dispose of enough electrical and electronic waste to equal the weight of 1,000,000 cars or 150,000 double-decker buses.

Figure 9.4 Landfill site

Working in groups, children list all the things they waste at home which end up in the general waste bin. Ask them to 'sort' their waste according to type or the material from which it is made. For example, food waste, garden waste, paper, plastic, glass, fabric, metal, and so on. Ask children to speculate about how much of that waste could be avoided. Probe their understanding of the problems with landfill and the reasons for recycling.

Installation Art! Pyramids of Garbage

Show the children Bahia Shahab's installation artwork 'Pyramids of Garbage'. Talk about its purpose. By creating the artwork in Cairo, close to the great pyramids of Giza, she is able to contrast some of mankind's greatest achievements with our present-day obsession with throw-away consumerism.

> As a species we have built monuments that have defeated time. We have designed civilizations that dreamt of eternity. With climate change, this eternity is now challenged. Now is the time for us to rethink our legacy on this planet. Are we going to come together to build a sustainable future for all of us or will our new legacy be pyramids of garbage?
>
> Bahia Shehab

Figure 9.5 Bahia Shehab's Pyramids of Garbage
Source: Credit: Bahia Shehab, Pyramid of Garbage, mixed media, 11mx6m, Garbage City, Cairo-Egypt

Working in groups, children plan and create their own art installation which draws attention to some of the problems waste is creating for the planet. They can start by researching appropriate art installations on the web. Organise an exhibition of the children's work for the local community.

Food waste

One thing children can do to safeguard the environment is to cut down on food waste, which on its own accounts for about 6% of the UK's carbon footprint. Talk about how most of our waste food ends up in landfill sites where it decomposes. Its carbon footprint is high because when food rots it emits large quantities of methane gas into the atmosphere. Also, the collection and transportation of food waste to the landfill sites produces further greenhouse emissions. Paint a picture in the children's minds depicting landfill sites as major emitters of greenhouse gas.

Art! Imagining the problem

Ask children to imagine what greenhouse gases would look like if they were visible to the human eye. Then ask them to paint a picture of a landfill site which depicts how the emissions are polluting the atmosphere. Remind the children that air is also a combination of gases, and this should also feature in their picture. Encourage them to describe how the emissions are contributing to the climate crisis. Listen to children's ideas and help them develop their understanding of the causes of the climate crisis. Use this activity as an opportunity to work on their understanding of the properties of gases.

Composting waste

Children can reduce the amount of rubbish sent to landfill by composting much of the school's organic waste. It may also be possible for some children to set up a compost bin at home. Explain that composting our waste produces less methane than landfill. This is because the waste decomposes in a different way, involving microorganisms which do not produce methane. Paper and card, if it can't be recycled, can also be composted. Things to put in the school compost bin include raw vegetables, fruits, eggshells, tea bags, weeds, dead leaves, straw, paper, and garden clippings. Leave out meat, fish, dairy, cooked food, and pet litter.

It is important to get the right balance in your bin. Green waste such as uncooked food and grass clippings should make up about 25–50%, while brown waste such as dry paper, dry leaves, and cardboard should make up the rest. A balanced mix ensures that enough air gets into the compost to prevent methane being produced and prevents a smelly compost heap.

Figure 9.6 Compostable wrapper

Enquire! Explore the compost heap

Children monitor the compost heap to discover the creatures that make it their home. Large numbers of woodlice can often be found in the compost heap, where they help decompose the waste. Woodlice are called detritivores because they feed on the detritus of decomposing vegetation. Other invertebrates such as slugs, snails, worms, and millipedes are also types of detritivores which can be found in a compost heap. A compost heap has its own ecosystem in which detritivores are primary consumers. Microorganisms such as bacteria and fungi are also primary consumers and play an important part in the composting process. Secondary and tertiary consumers include centipedes, springtails, and certain types of ants, beetles, and mites.

Children use information sources to learn about the different types of detritivores and other invertebrates that live in their compost heap. Help them create food chains and food webs to depict the ecology of their compost heap. Use images from the web to create a display. Link this with further work on living things and their habitats.

Figure 9.7 Compost bin and planter made from recycled drawers

Plastic waste

Waste is a problem for all of us, especially plastics, which take a long time to decompose. Plastic is a synthetic material, meaning it has been made by chemically changing another substance, in this case oil. The manufacture of plastics needs a lot of energy, mainly produced by burning fossil fuels. For example, 9 supermarket carrier bags require the equivalent energy, and therefore produce similar amounts of greenhouse gases, of driving a car a distance of 1 km. Before supermarkets charged for supplying bags, the UK used up to 20 billion plastic bags every year. Let the children do the maths to find the equivalent in car miles. That's a lot of energy and greenhouse gases and a lot of waste, which makes producing plastic unsustainable.

Vision! A waste-free world

Introduce children to World Cleanup Day, which in 2021 was held on 18th September. More than 5 million activists from 180 countries took part, and they cleaned up over 280,000 tonnes of waste. Ask children why they think World Cleanup Day is necessary. What were the activists trying to achieve? Talk about how it is a form of direct action towards achieving a vision of a waste-free world. Listen to children's ideas about whether a waste-free world will ever be possible. What can children do to help?

Working in groups, ask children to describe what a day without waste would be like. Their story should start from the time they get up in the morning until they go to bed at night. Groups come together to share their ideas with the rest of the class. Some children should act as waste detectives, and politely challenge the storytellers to justify activities which they think may not be waste-free. Vote on whether the class would like to take part in the next World Cleanup Day.

Enquire! Sustainable packaging

The main supermarkets have devised policies to make their packaging more eco-friendly by making more use of sustainable materials. Working in groups, children discuss the difference between materials which are sustainable and those which are unsustainable. Ask each group to identify five examples of supermarket products which involve the use of sustainable materials and five which use unsustainable ones, including packaging. Ask them to justify their choices. Listen to children's ideas and address misconceptions. Explain how we use the term 'sustainable' to describe materials and products that can be made and used with minimal damage to the planet. Single-use plastic products are unsustainable because their manufacture creates damaging greenhouse gases, and their use creates waste that pollutes the planet. When we describe a material or product as sustainable, we are saying that we can keep making it and using it for the foreseeable future without damaging the planet and adding to the climate crisis. Sustainable materials and products help ensure a secure and sustainable future!

Working in groups, children research and compare the plastics and packaging policies of the main supermarkets, to discover what they intend to do to reduce single-use

Figure 9.8 Food market in France

plastics. Even though the bulk of single-use plastic packaging is now recyclable, much of it still ends up in landfill. Ask children what they think supermarkets can do to reduce their reliance on single-use plastics. Children use supermarkets' online shopping websites to discover how different types of products are packaged, and identify those products which could possibly be packaged in a more sustainable way. Debate whether most vegetables require any packaging. What other products could be sold without packaging? Show children images of a range of traditional food markets with unpackaged fruit and veg on display. Talk about why the food isn't packaged. Debate why supermarkets package so many of their food products. Does packaging keep the food fresher, or does it help reduce the number of staff employed by the supermarket? Does it help make shopping easier and quicker? What would be the consequences for shoppers if supermarkets stopped packaging their food products? Based on their enquiry children, suggest ways of reducing plastic packaging in supermarkets.

Design! Eco-packaging

Talk to the children about eco-packaging. Can they find any examples at home or in school? Make a display of any available examples of eco-packaging. Define 'eco-packaging' as packaging that uses sustainable materials and manufacturing practices that have minimal impact on the climate. Working in groups, challenge children to design a range of eco-packaging products which could be used by supermarkets. Ask children to justify the materials and explain how their product will be used. Add children's designs to the eco-packaging display.

Enquire! Types of plastic

Plastics are not all the same, and the first process in recycling is to sort them into similar types. For this enquiry, children bring a range of clean waste plastic items into school. Provide each group with a number of different items. They should first sort them according to their uses. They then test the items to see if those with common uses have similar properties. The following are common tests used to identify plastics:

1. Translucency – light test.
2. Hardness – scratch test.
3. Flexibility – stiff or easy to bend without stressing.
4. Buoyancy – float or sink.
5. Stress marks – white marks on edges when cut.
6. Density – mass (grams) per unit volume (cubic centimetres).

Children record the results of their tests and use the outcomes to sort the plastics by their properties. They may need some help to measure the density. Children then use symbols on the items and information sources to identify the different types of plastics. Children find out which of their items are easy to recycle and which will most probably end up in landfill. Polyethylene Terephthalate (PET), which is used to make single-use clear plastic bottles, is the easiest and the most commonly recycled plastic. Look out for labels telling you how much of the plastic has already been recycled. How many companies claim their products are carbon neutral?

Figure 9.9 Label on recyclable bottle
Source: Anna Loxley

Figure 9.10 Label for clothing with recycled plastic bottles
Source: Anna Loxley

Story-telling! PET and the fashion world

Bring to school items of clothing or fabrics made partly using recycled polyester. Recycled polyester is made out of recycled plastic bottles. Talk together about the types of clothes children like to wear and whether they are made from recycled polyester. Children use information sources to tell the story of a clear plastic bottle from the time it is dropped in their recycling bin at home to the time it ends up as part of the fabric of a fashion item in a clothing store. Debate whether recycling plastic for clothing has a positive or negative impact on the climate crisis. Are there more environmentally-friendly fabrics which we can use? Challenge children to discover which type of fabric is most sustainable.

Visit a recycling plant

Organise a visit to a recycling plant to see how the waste plastic products are sorted and treated. If this is not possible, contact your local council to organise a visit to the school from an environmental education officer. In each case, plan the visit in advance with the children so they can prepare probing questions.

Campaign! Cut down on waste

Point out that 7 million tonnes of food are thrown away by households in the UK every year, which ends up rotting in landfill. In addition, we throw away close to 300 billion pieces of plastic, much of which is single-use. Children use information sources to plan a campaign to raise awareness among the school community of the problems caused by waste.

The campaign should be organised in two parts:

1. It should contain well-targeted information about the problems food and plastic waste create for the environment and wildlife.
2. Targeted, practical suggestions about what can be done to reduce everyday waste.

The campaign could include a video which is posted on the school's website or preferred social media platform. The video could highlight some of the things the children are doing, such as composting food waste, wastepaper, and garden waste. They could also include in the video an audit of the amount of single-use plastic their families use in a week and practical suggestions about how it could be reduced.

Information sources

Websites

- Carbon footprints, food miles, carbon saving, healthy diet, air miles, make do and mend
- How much does your school waste? | Recycle Now
- How plastics contribute to climate change – Yale Climate Connections
- Invertebrates of the Compost Pile – Cornell Composting
- Kids Against Plastic
- Kids Can Save The Planet
- Lilly Platt: Meet Earth.Org's First Global Ambassador! | Earth.Org – Past | Present | Future
- Meet generation Greta: young climate activists around the world | Environmental activism | The Guardian
- Plastic waste and climate change – what's the connection? – WWF-Australia – WWF-Australia
- Pyramids of Garbage – Bahia Shehab
- Recycling in Schools | Guidance on Reducing Waste (highspeedtraining.co.uk)
- Single-use plastics a serious climate change hazard, study warns | Environment | The Guardian
- UK throws away 295 billion pieces of plastic waste a year, report estimates | ITV News
- World Cleanup Day
- Young Scotswoman of the Year Holly Gillibrand: 'Caring is not enough – we have to act' | Glasgow Times

Working on scientific understanding

The first step in reducing our carbon footprint is to understand it. In this part, children work on their understanding of their carbon footprint and explore ways to reduce it. Start this part by reminding children that their carbon footprint is a measure of the impact that their activities have on the climate. Refer to information in Part 1 to help explain how their carbon footprint is determined.

Analyse! Carbon footprint

Challenge children to speculate about whether a banana (110g CO2e) has a larger or smaller carbon footprint than a cheeseburger (3.2Kg CO2e). Encourage them to analyse all the processes involved in producing different foods. For example, bananas are grown in natural sunlight and transported by boat, which is about 1% of the carbon footprint of air freight. They can also be sold without packaging, as they are wrapped by nature. According to Berners-Lee, bananas are a great food for anyone who cares about their carbon footprint, and of course they are good for children's health.

On the other hand, cheeseburgers are not so healthy, and have a whopping great carbon footprint. This is because burgers and cheese come from cows, which are one of the main producers of greenhouse gases. Intensive farming practices also add their footprint, as do processing, transport, and packaging. Mike Berners-Lee's book *How Bad Are Bananas* provides the carbon footprints for most everyday things, and is an invaluable aid when teaching this topic.

Evaluate! Carbon footprint

Start by showing children a chart of a person's average annual carbon footprint (Figure 9.11). Point out that the average total footprint is 12.7 tonnes CO2e, which is far too high. To play our part in achieving net zero emissions, we all need to drastically reduce our emissions to close to 5 tonnes.

To help understand their carbon footprint, children classify their sources of emissions into four categories: food, travel, home, and everything else. For example, in the food section they include the different types of food they eat at school, home, and when they eat out. In the travel section, they enter the type of transport they normally use, as well as longer distances for visits and holidays. Emissions at home include energy used for heating, lighting, and cooking, and everything else includes non-food shopping, use of mobile phones, leisure activities, and so on. Working in groups, children compare and discuss how they could reduce their carbon emissions. Use Mike Berners-Lee's book *How Bad Are Bananas* to estimate children's footprints for a day. Children can use a carbon calculator such as *My Footprint* from the WWF to evaluate their family's carbon footprint.

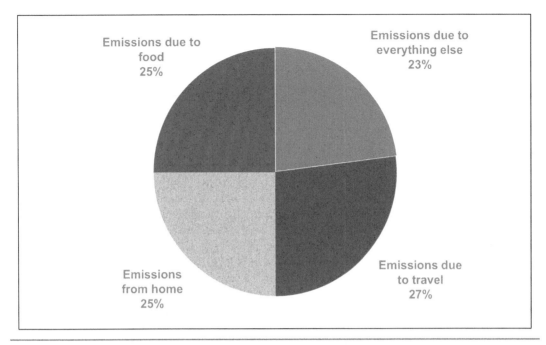

Figure 9.11 A person's average annual carbon footprint living in the UK

Information taken from Berners-Lee, How Bad Are Bananas?

Enquire! Reduce emissions from food

Start by reminding children of the need to eat a healthy diet. Point out that it's not only good for them, but is also good for the planet because a healthy diet can help reduce their carbon footprint. Use suitable illustrations to talk about the five main food groups, which are fruit and vegetables, starchy foods, dairy, proteins, and fats. Link the following activities to the work you do on healthy eating.

Talk about the food children eat and how much energy has to go into transporting it to them. Point out that 25% of greenhouse emissions come from the production and transportation of food in the UK. For example, a packet of oven-cooked chips involves farming the potatoes and oil, transporting them in trucks, planes or ships, processing and packaging, transporting the chips to shops and supermarkets, and lighting and heating the supermarkets where they are sold. Also, shopping by car and cooking the chips in the oven adds to their footprint.

Ask children to list all the things they ate yesterday, and classify them under the following headings: meat, fruit, bread, vegetables, dairy, sweets, and other things. Encourage them to speculate about the foods with the largest carbon footprint.

Questionnaire! Food miles

Where we get our food from matters, but how that food is produced and how it gets to us matters even more. For example, which do you think would have the largest footprint: strawberries grown in Spain or those grown in the UK? According to research commissioned by the Woodland Trust, strawberries grown on a farm in Scotland had a larger footprint than a similar type grown in Spain. The reason is that much of the fruit grown out of season in the UK is grown in energy-intensive hothouses. However, by rule of thumb, food which is air-freighted will arrive in the UK with a relatively huge carbon footprint, compared to shipped and locally produced seasonal produce.

Talk to children about where their food comes from. Do they know which of their food is produced locally? Point out that locally produced food is likely to involve fewer carbon emissions. With this in mind, children plan a questionnaire to find where local supermarkets source their meat, fruit, and vegetables. The questions should relate to particular types of meat, fruit, and vegetables, and where the supermarkets source them at different times of the year. Children work on the questionnaire in groups, and then come together to share their ideas. Having agreed on a final version, children send the questionnaire to the managers of all the supermarkets in their area, with an invitation to visit the school and talk about what the company is doing to reduce its carbon footprint. Children report the outcomes of the questionnaire on the school website or preferred social media platform. Create a huge map of the world in the classroom showing where commonly eaten foods come from at different times of the year. Children use a carbon calculator on the web to produce a footprint for each of the foods on the map.

Debate! Carbon saving guidelines

Talk about whether children should consider their carbon footprint when they have a choice in what they eat. Discuss how often children eat everything that is bought for them and how often they use leftovers to make other meals. Do they know which foods they eat are air-freighted and which are produced locally? And do they make an effort to choose foods that can be bought without packaging? How much plastic do they throw away as a result of their food shopping? Remind children that the production of plastic produces huge amounts of greenhouse gases. Talk about the consumption of beef, lamb, and dairy products as major contributors to their footprints. Remind children of the methane that ruminators add to the atmosphere. For more information about methane from farm animals, refer to Chapter 5.

Working in groups, children discuss realistic ways they could reduce their food footprint. Groups come together to share ideas and debate what they think is possible, considering their lifestyle. Compare children's ideas with the following set of guidelines devised by Berners-Lee to cut our food footprint by half. Children debate whether Berners-Lee's proposals are feasible for them and their families.

1. Eat less meat and dairy (especially beef and lamb).
2. Eat everything you buy. Learn to enjoy eating leftovers.
3. Avoid air-freighted food.
4. Try to reduce packaging.

More information can be found in Berners-Lee (2020)

Working within the guidelines! Footprint Friday

At the beginning of a week, groups plan what they will eat on Friday to reduce their carbon footprints. Choose another day if Friday presents a cultural problem for some children in your class. Point out this is a realistic attempt to follow these rules and reduce their greenhouse gas emissions. Groups start by listing the things they would normally eat on Friday, and using carbon calculators identify those with the highest footprints. Groups should explore which items of their normal Friday food are probably air-freighted, and which items come ready-packaged.

When planning their Footprint Friday meals, children should avoid beef and lamb, and choose alternative forms of protein. Fish is traditionally eaten by some people on Friday but can be expensive. Suggest they try tasty 'veggie' alternatives. Make it clear that the food they choose should be affordable and provide them with a healthy balanced diet.

By the end of the exercise, all the children should have planned their Friday meals and have some idea about the extent to which they reduced their carbon footprint. Ask children to justify their choice of foods with regard to providing a healthy diet and at the same time reducing their footprint. If possible, involve families in the project so that the children are able to purchase their choice of food and enjoy eating it on the Friday. Perhaps some of the families could be persuaded to reduce their food footprints!

Finally, groups discuss the problems which may prevent them following the carbon-saving guidelines devised by Berners-Lee. Which would they be prepared to follow? Organise a class summit to discuss what the children would be prepared/able to do to reduce their carbon footprints.

Discuss! Sustainable diet

Children visit the Livewell web pages to discover more about the changes needed in food production and diet to limit global warming. Working in groups, they discuss the six Livewell principles for healthy and sustainable food. How could these principles be modified to appeal to children of their own age? What normally influences their food choices? Talk about the practical problems. Groups produce posters designed to inform and persuade their peers to adopt a sustainable diet. Encourage them to think of catchy titles for their posters to appeal to their age group.

Design! Carbon labelling

Before buying a food product, carbon labelling is a way to identify the impact the product has on the climate. With the right information, labelling can help people make better choices to reduce their carbon footprints. Bring into school a range of food products for which children can design and make carbon labels. Children create a simple fact-sheet on carbon labelling, which can be published on the school website or in the newsletter.

Figure 9.12 Carbon footprint symbols

Reduce! Emissions due to travel

Talk about how travel accounts for about 27% of their carbon footprints. Children discuss the different ways they travel during the year. Point out that travelling by car and flying contribute most to their footprints. The most obvious way children can reduce their travel footprints is to walk or cycle to school, or use public transport instead of the car. Survey the class to find out how the children travel to school, and display the results. Talk together about the viability of using alternative ways of travelling to reduce their carbon footprints. Identify and discuss any problems, and debate solutions.

Arrange for children to visit other classes in the school to discover how they travel to school and add the data to the display. Talk about the ways the school could reduce its travel footprint. Groups discuss whether cycling, walking, or using public transport to school are possible for all the children. What about the teachers and other staff? What can be done to persuade more children (and parents) to cut their travel footprints? Groups come together to decide what they think can be done. They could organise a questionnaire to discover the views of other children in the school.

Reduce! Air travel

Talk about how aeroplanes emit huge amounts of greenhouse gases. Ask children what they could do to persuade people to fly less. Do they think people would be prepared to holiday closer to home and travel by train to reduce their carbon footprints?

Figure 9.13 Symbolic shadow of aeroplane

Working in groups, children create travel brochures designed to persuade people to holiday closer to home rather than flying long distances. 'Closer to home' means destinations which can be reasonably reached by train travel, such as places in the UK or parts of Europe. The brochures should promote the value of train travel and the destinations as attractive places for family holidays.

Reduce! Emissions at home

Talk about the contribution home heating and the use of electrical appliances can make to the children's carbon footprints. Ask them to list all the ways they use energy at home. Groups use carbon calculators to discover the biggest emitters. Children discuss and agree on a list of 10 practical 'can-do' ways of reducing their home footprint.

Reduce! Lifestyle emissions

Ask children how they think their lifestyles increase their carbon footprints. As an example, ask them how often they buy new jeans, and to imagine how much a pair of jeans adds to their carbon footprint. Over their lifetime, a pair of cotton jeans can add as much as 32Kg CO_2e to a footprint. Just a new pair of jeans adds 19Kg CO_2e due to manufacture and transport, and then washing and drying can add the rest. Children use carbon calculators to discover which of their clothes have the largest footprints. Do clothes made from natural materials have smaller footprints than synthetics?

Poster campaign! Make do and mend

Talk about when clothes were rationed in the Second World War; during the war, people had to extend the life of their clothes by repairing them and washing them more carefully. In those difficult times people had to 'make do and mend', which was an attitude that applied to most things. Today, the slogan 'reduce, reuse, recycle' is often used to encourage people to reduce waste.

Ask the children what they would be prepared to do to support the effort to combat the climate crisis. Would they be prepared to make do and mend? Here's what Berners-Lee suggests could be done:

1. Buy stuff that is easy to wash and dry
2. Buy stuff that is built to last, wear it, repair it, and use it until it falls apart (or pass it on)
3. Buy second-hand
4. Donate or recycle clothing rather than putting it in the bin
5. Favour synthetic fibres over natural ones (because they last longer)

Working in groups, children plan their own 'make do and mend' poster campaign to persuade the school community to take action against climate change. They can get ideas by exploring the 'make do and mend' campaign posters produced during war years. Children can plan their campaign around clothing or any other lifestyle items, such as

Figure 9.14 Bag made from recycled jeans

toys, which are often discarded for newer models. The campaigns should each have their own slogans and a clear focus on reducing the size of the community's carbon footprint. Groups present their campaigns at a school assembly.

Make! Patchwork

Children can learn sewing skills so they can repair their own clothes. Start by making patchwork quilts. Patchwork quilts were historically the ultimate example of reusing in action. Children can also make rag rugs or patchwork stuffed toys, like Elmer, for younger classes. Alternatively, ask children to bring in well-worn, old clothes which can be darned, patched, shortened, or altered to be repurposed or to extend their life.

The Repair Shop

Show children parts of TV programmes such as *The Repair Shop* and *Money for Nothing* that repair and upcycle old and damaged products. Working in groups, children choose an item to upcycle, repurpose, or repair, and make a video of their work in the style of one of the popular TV shows.

Information sources

Websites

- BBC – WW2 People's War – MAKE DO AND MEND
- How Bad Are Bananas?
- How to calculate your carbon footprint: How bad are bananas? | Tom Church
- The resurgence of product carbon footprint labelling | Carbon Trust
- What is a carbon footprint? | Greenhouse gas emissions | The Guardian
- WWF Footprint Calculator

Books

- Berners-Lee, M. (2020) *How Bad Are Bananas*? London: Profile books Ltd.
- Berners-Lee, M. (2019) *There Is No Planet B*. Cambridge: Cambridge University Press.
- Masters, M. (2020) *123 Seriously Smart Things You Need to Know about Climate*. London: Thames and Hudson.

The bigger picture

In this part, children look at ways of reducing their carbon footprints by capturing carbon dioxide from the air and locking it away in plants, which also benefits local wildlife struggling from the effects of the climate crisis. Opportunities are also provided for children to become involved in citizen science projects.

Greening-up the school

Use ideas from Chapter 8 and the first part of this chapter to talk about the ways children could green-up the school to help reduce their carbon footprints. Remind them how trees play an important part in carbon capture, because their size enables them to store large amounts of carbon.

Children should consider planting trees and other plants which provide additional benefits, as well as sequestering carbon. For example, growing fruit trees and vegetable plants not only removes carbon from the air, but can also be used to supplement the food used for school meals. Talk about how using homegrown food reduces the school's carbon footprint because it cuts down on transport emissions. Growing hedging plants instead of building fences provides an additional way to capture carbon. For most schools the reduction in their footprint may be small, but by greening-up all our schools, the combined contribution to addressing the climate crisis could be considerable.

Working in groups, children survey the school grounds to identify space for growing plants. Talk about how varieties of apple and other fruit trees can be grown directly in the ground, up the sides of buildings, or in containers. If ground space is limited, most vegetables can be grown in containers. Children should also consider growing some perennial plants in beds alongside their vegetables, as the roots store carbon throughout the year. As a result of the survey, groups draw up plans for greening-up the school, which includes a planting scheme for maximum sequestration. Groups come together to share their ideas and agree on a planting scheme. Integrate planting the garden with the curriculum work on plants.

Create a butterfly garden

Use information from Part 1 to talk about creating a butterfly garden. Describe how butterflies have been hard hit by the climate crisis. Ask children to describe and talk about their favourite types of butterflies. How many species can they identify? Children use information sources to discover more about their local butterflies and whether they are in decline or belong to the few species that are thriving. In 2021, Butterfly Conservation ran a project to map the arrival of the Painted Lady and other migrant insects. Encourage children to explore the results of the survey and find out whether climate change is having an impact on the numbers of migrant insects visiting the UK.

Children can visit the Butterfly Conservation website to discover how to build a garden to attract butterflies onto the school grounds. Gardens can be essential fuelling stations for insects, where they can get an energy boost as they travel between nature reserves and other natural habitats. Schools don't need lots of space to provide a stop-off point for butterflies. Well-stocked containers in sunny positions can create a 'nectar bar' where butterflies and other insects can stop off to refuel. Plants such as lavender, marjoram, and wallflowers do well in containers, while verbena and buddleia can be grown in a sunny position near a fence. Try to fill every available space with plants to maximise carbon capture and provide homes and food for a wide range of butterflies and other insects.

In spring and autumn, children record the types and numbers of butterflies that visit the school garden and compare their findings with national surveys published on the web. It is important to note the sighting of the first butterfly of the year, to find out whether butterflies are active before the 'nectar bar' is in full bloom. Emerging early not only puts insects out of sync with the plants; it also affects other animals in their ecosystem who depend on the insects for food. From this point of view, children can analyse the impact changing weather patterns are having on the garden ecosystem. Link this part with curriculum work on living things and their habitats.

Citizen science

If children have not been involved before, introduce children to the idea of citizen science. Explain that citizen science is an opportunity for the children to get involved in a real science project, which is organised by practicing scientists. The results of their work can contribute to the success of national and international research projects about the impact of climate change on the environment and wildlife.

Big Butterfly Count

The Big Butterfly Count is a UK-wide survey organised by Butterfly Conservation. The purpose of the survey is to assess the health of our environment by simply counting and identifying the different types of butterflies and moths that we see. In 2021, data was collected over 15-minute observation periods between 16th July and 8th August. The data collected is compared by scientists to previous surveys to assess the health of our butterfly and moth populations.

Figure 9.15 Observing butterflies close-up

Chris Packham, wildlife broadcaster and vice-president of Butterfly Conservation, explains the importance of the count with regard to monitoring the impact of the climate crisis:

> Because butterflies and moths make excellent indicators of the impacts of climate change and other human environmental factors, collecting data on their numbers is really important. So, something as simple as recording a butterfly spotted in your garden, at your local park or on your window box can play a part in vital research into a global problem. It's a really valuable contribution everyone can make.

The Big Butterfly Count provides opportunities for children to be involved in an important nationwide project, and at the same time further develop their understanding of the impact the climate crisis is having on our wildlife. All the information you need, including learning resources, can be downloaded from the Butterfly Conservation website.

The Garden Butterfly Survey

The Garden Butterfly Survey is another nationwide project organised by Butterfly Conservation to monitor the health of the butterfly population. This survey is ongoing and children can submit sightings of butterflies in their gardens at home, or in the school garden, throughout the year. The project complements the Big Butterfly Count, providing additional data concerning the impact of climate change on the life cycles of the butterflies. Information and resources can be found on the Butterfly Conservation website.

Nature's Calendar Project

The Nature's Calendar Project is organised by the Woodland Trust. Its purpose is to track the effects of weather and climate change on wildlife in different parts of the country. Children can join the project and help scientists discover the effects climate change is having on the environment near you. By joining the project, children will contribute to a biological record that dates back as far as 1736.

The Big Garden Birdwatch

The Big Garden Birdwatch Project is organised by the Royal Society for the Protection of Birds (RSPB). The purpose of this long-running project is to monitor the numbers of different species of birds that visit our gardens. By comparing their numbers with previous years, the scientists can work out which birds are thriving during the climate crisis, and which are in decline.

The Wildlife Trusts

The Wildlife Trusts have a mission to restore a third of the UK's land and seas for the conservation of nature by 2030. No matter where you live in the UK, there is a Wildlife

Figure 9.16 Shells and plastic waste found on the beach

Trust standing up for wildlife and wild places. Each Trust is formed by people from many different backgrounds, acting together to protect the natural world and to tackle the climate crisis. The Wildlife Trusts rely on citizen science projects to gather a wide range of data on wildlife populations, habitats, and behaviours. Visit the Wildlife Trusts website for your area to discover their current citizen science projects. Here are two examples of projects which were current in 2021:

Shoresearch project: This is a national survey of the intertidal shore around the UK. By signing up to this project, children will learn to identify shoreline plants and wildlife and help to monitor this special habitat. The data collected from this project helps experts to monitor our fragile sea life and better understand the effects of pollution, climate change, and invasive alien species.

Hedgehog citizen science: Wildlife Trusts in different areas such as Wiltshire, Devon, and Cumbria invite volunteers to become a *Hedgehog Hero* by helping them survey and protect the population of this well-loved creature, which is now vulnerable to extinction.

Information sources

Websites

- A Round-Up of Citizen Science Wildlife Projects – Wild Ideas (wild-ideas.org.uk)
- Butterfly-Conservation-Strategy Brochure.pdf
- Shoresearch | The Wildlife Trusts

- Citizen science | Natural History Museum (nhm.ac.uk)
- Citizen science projects | The Wildlife Trusts
- BBC – Do Something Great – Citizen science
- Big Butterfly Count | BBC Wildlife Magazine – Discover Wildlife
- https://gardenbutterflysurvey.org
- Home page | Butterfly Conservation (butterfly-conservation.org)
- Gardening Basics: Carbon Cycle and Carbon Sequestration – KidsGardening
- A Global Garden: Plants Storing Carbon (nasa.gov)
- Carbon Farming: Sequestering Carbon in Plants and Soil – ethical.net
- Big Garden Birdwatch | The RSPB
- Nature's Calendar (woodlandtrust.org.uk)
- Gardening for Climate Change/RHS Campaign for School Gardening
- Fast growing trees for your garden – Woodland Trust
- How Trees Fight Climate Change – Woodland Trust

Books

- Loxley, P. (2021) *Big Ideas in Outdoor Primary Science*. Abingdon: Routledge.

The last word

It is only right that the last word in this book should belong to young climate activists who continue to remind governments and other decision-makers that the time for talking has passed, the science evidence is clear, and actions are needed to solve the climate crisis. Here is an extract from an article published in the New York Times in August 2021. The authors are youth climate activists from Sweden, Mexico, Bangladesh, and Kenya. This is what they had to say:

> Millions of young people have united in a movement with one voice, demanding that decision-makers do the work necessary to save our planet from unprecedented heat waves, massive floods and vast wildfires we are increasingly witnessing. Our protest will not end until the inaction does.
>
> Climate change is the single greatest threat to our futures. We are the ones who will have to clean up the mess you adults have made, and we are the ones who are more likely to suffer now. Children are more vulnerable than adults to the dangerous weather events, diseases and other harms caused by climate change.
>
> Greta Thunberg, Adriana Calderon,
Farzana Faruk Jhumu, and Eric Njuguna

Mitigation and adaptation

carbon capture · renewable energy · biomass boiler · seed bank ·
upcycling · rewilding · solar power · green roof · permeable paving ·
wind farm · sequestration · cycle lane · electric car · re-purposing ·
coastal defences · carbon sink · mitigation · reforestation ·
ethical investment · eco building · composting · green tariffs ·
energy-saving lights · insulation · waste management · re-usable bags ·
clothes swop · no-dig · sustainable materials · responsible sourcing ·
conservation · supporting biodiversity · behavioural change ·
shelter belts · green corridors · thermal heat pumps · peat-free compost ·
naturalisation · retrofitting · water management · recycling ·
edible landscapes · protein substitutes · solar reflectors · plant-based diet ·
ocean clean-up · tree planting · adaptation · creating wetlands ·
Fair Trade goods · flood management · green hydrogen · beach clean ·
wind turbines · offsetting · flood risk management · locally-produced ·
urban greening · saving sea grass · eco-friendly products · carbon store ·
city trees · reducing emissions · water-wise gardening · food security ·
plastic substitutes · pollution abatement · planting kelp forests ·
eco-engineering · xeriscaping · front yard farming · soil health ·
longer product lifetime · responsible consumption · less mowing ·
make do and mend · less flying · compostable packaging ·
supporting the poorest and most vulnerable to climate change ·
green industrial revolution · zero carbon · jet zero · NET ZERO ·

INDEX

Note: Page numbers in *italics* indicate a figure and page numbers in **bold** indicate a table on the corresponding page.

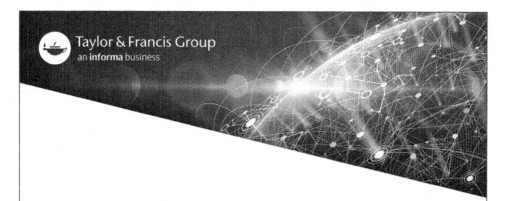